Lees-Milne. James

VENETIAN EVENINGS

James Lees-Milne

VENETIAN
EVENINGS

COLLINS
8 Grafton Street London W1
1988

William Collins Sons & Co. Ltd
London · Glasgow · Sydney · Auckland
Toronto · Johannesburg

British Library Cataloguing in Publication Data

Lees-Milne, James
    Venetian evenings.
    1. Architecture——Italy——Venice
    ——History   2. Venice (Italy)——
    Buildings
    I. Title
    720'.945'31   NA1121.V4

    ISBN 0 00 217937 7

First published 1988
Copyright © James Lees-Milne 1988

Set in Linotron Baskerville at The Spartan Press Ltd,
Lymington, Hants
Made and printed in Great Britain by
T.J. Press (Padstow) Ltd, Padstow, Cornwall

FOR ALVIDE

who is always in a hurry

CONTENTS

ILLUSTRATIONS

Oh Venice! Venice! when thy marble walls
Are level with the waters, there shall be
A cry of nations o'er thy sunken halls,
A loud lament along the sweeping sea!

> BYRON, 'Ode on Venice'

The history of Venice reads like a romance; the
place seems a fantastic vision at the best, from
which the world must at last awake some morning,
and find that after all it has only been dreaming,
and that there never was any such city.

> W. D. HOWELLS, *Venetian Life*

It is great pleasure to write the word; but I am not
sure there is not a certain impudence in pretending to
add anything to it.   HENRY JAMES, *Italian Hours*

PREFACE

Few people, I think, would dispute that Venice is an autumnal, a sunset city. By this I do not necessarily mean it is so because the days of its glory lie in the past – an argument, architecturally speaking, which applies to practically every ancient city – but because it is best seen in late afternoons just before twilight. Great artists have found this out. Great writers have repeatedly dwelt on it. Théophile Gautier on reaching the Piazza wrote, '*Le soleil couchant illumine du rose le plus vif la façade de Saint-Marc, qui semble rougir et scintille ardemment dans ce dernier rayon.*' With that Gallic love of hyperbole he emphasizes the point that all the buildings of Venice, when bathed in shadow, the light behind them, assume azure, lilac and violet tones

> on which is etched in black the rigging of buildings riding at anchor; above them explodes a blaze of splendour, a firework display of rays of light; the sun sets in a mass of topaz rubies, amethysts, all constantly moving as the wind changes the shapes of the clouds; dazzling rockets shoot up between the two cupolas of the Salute, and sometimes – depending on where one is standing – Palladio's spire cuts the sun's disc in two.

Which is undoubtedly very lovely. But what enhances the magic of the spectacle is that the buildings are reflected in water. A Venetian sunset, more magnificent than that of any other kind, has the Lagoon for a mirror. The campanile of San Giorgio Maggiore gives the impression of having its foundations at the bottom of an abyss. The duplicated tower seems to swim between two skies, or two seas. Is it the water, Gautier asks, which reflects the sky, or the sky the water? The eye hesitates to pronounce and everything is confronted in a general '*éblouissement*'.

Henry James, whom I quote rather often in the following pages – how refreshing are the observant man of letters' impressions of buildings after the dry-as-dust factual descriptions of the architectural historian – was equally sunset-struck. 'I came into Venice', he wrote in 1909, 'just as I had done before, toward the end of a summer day, when the shadows begin to lengthen and the light to glow, and found that the attendant sensations bore repetition remarkably well.' And again, in reminiscing upon an ancient palace,

> If in the absence of its masters you have happened to have it to yourself for twenty-four hours you will never forget the charm of its haunted stillness, late on the summer afternoon for instance, when the call of playing children comes in behind from the *campo*, nor the way the old ghosts seemed to pass on tip-toe on the marble floors.

This is all very well, you will be saying, but it is well known that Venetian churches are best seen before midday when they close, some for good; and the light in those that don't close is in the afternoon too bad for sight-seeing. To which my lame reply is that more and more churches do re-open after 3.30 or 4 p.m., when in summer the light is often better than in the morning. In any case the façades, as Gautier and James have attested, look their mellowest in the evenings.

By explaining what this book is *not* I run the risk of deterring readers. So, to be brief, let me candidly point out that it is not a guidebook to, nor a history of, nor an architectural treatise on Venice. It consists of discursive essays, or as I prefer to think them, undelivered lectures, on eleven monuments, taken more or less in chronological order. The monuments are chosen arbitrarily in that they are among my favourite buildings; they may not be among the favourites of others. In making my selection I had difficulty. It was precisely sixty years ago that I paid my first visit to Venice and I do not think there is a single monument that I have not at some time or another seen and looked at with attention. There are few that I do not deeply love. However, for good or ill, the eleven I have selected represent different periods of Venetian architecture, save the late nineteenth and the twentieth centuries. Without prejudice I do not think that there are many buildings from 1850 to the present day that count for much in the Venetian context.

What the book means to be is a help and stimulus to those people who may not be architectural scholars but are interested in what Venice has to offer in buildings, to those people who find themselves there for the first time. Often I have been asked by friends about to pay their first visit, 'What buildings ought I to see within a week to ten days?' I hope this book may give an answer and whet their appetite for further and deeper explorations and studies.

The reason why I have included only two palaces is not because I prefer ecclesiastical to domestic architecture. Far from it. It is simply because there are very few palaces open to the public, and, as far as I know, not one privately owned and inhabited from top to bottom. Even the richest Venetian families nowadays confine themselves to a single floor, where understandably they are disinclined to admit strangers. Not that admittance was often granted when a family occupied a whole palace, as readers of *The Aspern Papers* will have gathered. The Ca' Rezzonico, that superbly furnished museum, indicates how many of the old palaces have been gutted of their original ceiling paintings, stuccoed and damask-hung walls and contents. I venture to guess that were we to gain access to them we would be shocked to find how little had been spared by the antique dealers and foreign millionaire collectors. This traffic in Venetian palace interiors has been in full swing for a very long time. Even in 1820 the Englishman W. J. Bankes was, with his friend the poet Byron's connivance, purchasing the famous *Judgement of Solomon* by Sebastiano del Piombo, and in the 1830s ripping out a ceiling canvas from the Palazzo Contarini degli Scrigni to adorn his country house in Dorset.

My book is a sort of anthology in that I have quoted extensively from earlier travellers to Venice, beginning with Fynes Moryson, who was in Venice in 1594. A reliable but prosaic chronicler, he was not gifted with much imagination or apparent enthusiasm for works of art. His near contemporary Thomas Coryate, on the other hand, was passionately interested in everything he saw, if not always very discriminating. His *Crudities* of 1611 are a delight. Coryate made a special journey to Venice in 1608 from his father's vicarage at Odcombe in Somerset, on foot. He walked back again, noting precisely that he had covered 952 miles, and hung up his shoes in the church as a sort of thanks-offering. He is one of the earliest Englishmen to record detailed impressions of what he called 'the more glorious, peerless, and maiden city of Venice: I call it maiden, because it was never conquered'. He is seldom boring or dull. He is curious, observant of the unusual, funny or odd. He was constantly measuring columns and church piers by throwing his arms round them, and expressing surprise, never disappointment, over their girth. He visited the Ghetto and attended a synagogue. The Levite that read the Law to the congregation, he wrote, from an exceedingly long scroll of parchment, rolled up on two wooden handles, pronounced 'before the congregation not by a sober, distinct, and orderly reading, but by an exceedingly loud yaling, undecent roaring, and as it were a beastly bellowing of it forth'. One can picture his amazement and amusement.

How different to Coryate's enthusiasms are John Ruskin's disparagements of nearly everything we like. I say *nearly* with emphatic qualification, since it is not becoming for us to sneer at Ruskin because he loathed and despised all classical architecture without exception, thought Claude Lorraine a second-rate painter and Poussin worthless. Within his Gothic limitations Ruskin is incomparable, *sui generis*. Probably no man has spent more effort noticing buildings and works of art, not even Bernard Berenson or Kenneth Clark. No man has written with more profound understanding of the medieval artists' and craftsmen's creations, and the motives that impelled them to work for their own as well as their Creator's glory. No man has described the moods of Venice in summer or winter, radiance or gloom, in more poetic and God-inspired prose. When we occasionally smile at him let us always remember that even at his silliest he had something worthy of our profound attention to say.

Heeding the warnings of wise Henry James, I have endeavoured to eschew in my text purple passages and all superfluous superlatives. I have also tried to be sparing with the names of lesser-known Venetian artists and sculptors, which tend to bore the uninitiated (like myself). Of sculptors medieval and early Renaissance, beyond the Buon (or Bon), the Lombardi, and of course giants like Sansovino and Vittoria, very little is known. Art historians are beginning to investigate these lacunae in our learning so as to attribute tombs and effigies to individuals. Whenever a name appears more than once I have thought fit to record it so that the reader may compare that sculptor's several works.

I am aware of the inconsistency over the names of Venetian monuments and places. Whereas reference to St Mark's as San Marco seems to me as pedantic as calling St Peter's Rome, San Pietro, yet I name the Golden House the Ca' d'Oro. It would surely be absurd to call La Madonna dell'Orto Our Lady of the Orchard, or Santa Maria della Salute St Mary of the Salvation. Similarly, essential Venetian terms seem best left in Italian, like *squero* for gondola's building yard, *campo* for square and *rio* for little canal. The glossary at the end of the book of some Italian words and some English architectural terms used in the text may prove helpful.

Finally I recommend that for English-speaking people about to spend more than a few days in Venice Hugh Honour's *Companion Guide to Venice* (Collins) is absolutely indispensable; and even if they can spare only one day they will do well to read the first chapter.

J. L-M.
1987

TORCELLO

639–1008

AD 452 is accepted as the birth year of Venice. Attila, King of the Huns, known to the Christian world as 'the Scourge of God', overran Aquileia, a Roman frontier fortress and important city on the river Natisone at the head of the Adriatic. After centuries of assault from Vandals, Goths, Visigoths, Gedpidae and other species of barbarians, this devastation was the penultimate straw (the Lombards were yet to come) that broke the backs of the Roman inhabitants of Venetia. Those who managed to escape the Hunnish sword fled literally into the water. Their only refuge was the lagoons, what Alcuin, the York-born adviser of the Emperor Charlemagne, was to call *'refugium in periculis'*. The wretched citizens of an ancient civilization were obliged to weave for themselves wattle shanties on the mud banks which over the millenniums had been deposited by the rivers Brenta, Sile and Piave. For a precarious living they turned to fishing and trading in salt. Whenever a lull in the barbarian incursions happened they stealthily returned to the mainland. Finally in 568 a Lombard invasion of the surviving towns and villages of Venetia decided the Roman community to abandon all hope of remaining on the mainland.

With a proficiency and industry born of misfortune the lagoon people soon established twelve townships in the several islands, governed by tribunes, or officers. But this form of government did not prove successful owing to jealousies and the desire of each township to be pre-eminent. So in 697 the first *dux* or doge was elected to rally the lagoon people under one banner against attack from outside. The tribunes were subjected to the doge, whose successors gradually brought the

17

lagoon people to dwell on the largest and most unassailable group of islets, the Rialto, where collectively they repulsed further incursions of Lombards and then Franks. In 810 a treaty with the Eastern Empire recognized the Venetians as territorial subjects of distant and ineffective Byzantium, while owing spiritual allegiance to the pope of Rome. Throughout their history they cunningly managed to play off the one authority against the other.

You may consider it strange and tiresome advice on the very first day after your arrival in Venice to take the public boat to Torcello. But there is a reason for it. Torcello is the cradle of Venice. From the Fondamenta Nuove, a long quayside at the north-west extremity of Venice, you sail into the Lagoon across the Canal dei Marani. The boat skirts the long brick wall of the island of San Michele, which is the city's cemetery. Only very renowned citizens or visitors – chiefly the latter – who have deigned to die in Venice are allowed to rest there in perpetuity. Ordinary folk are boxed in shelves within mortuary chapels, or merely within honey-comb apertures, for twelve years, after which time – approximately coincident with the soul's sojourn in Purgatory – they are emptied from their coffins and taken unceremoniously in barges to the island of Costanziaca and there jettisoned. So congested is this island, which receives very little notoriety, that the skeletons overflow into the Lagoon. Frederick Rolfe, Baron Corvo, leaning from his *sandalo*, claimed to have seen sea serpents issuing from the eye-sockets of skulls.

Leaving the snowy white chapel and the blue grey cypresses of San Michele we head for Murano, passing on our left a range of plain warehouses and one long building which might be the Banqueting Hall at Whitehall, it is so meticulously Palladian. We then catch a glimpse of the Grand Canal of Murano, a *campo*, a campanile, some old houses on the water – a miniature Venice. Next, along the shingle a drift of the plastic trash that afflicts the whole Lagoon and is indissoluble. Then glass factories, and the name Salviati in large gold lettering. On our far right is the thin pencil line of San Erasmo, which from the boat looks an inviting island of woods, orchards and green fields. Then San Francesco del Deserto, the property of the

Friars of the Madonna dell'Orto, where for days and even winter nights on end Baron Corvo, absolutely impoverished and starving, hitched his *sandalo*.

The boat gathers speed along the open avenue bounded by bunches of *pali* (stakes) like giant asparagus stalks, three or even five to a bunch. Some have an electrified lantern stuck on a projecting stick. Individual seagulls stand, king-of-the-castle-like, on the un-electrified *pali*, seeming not to care for the electrified ones. An overtaking motor-boat will cut a green swathe of wash across our bows. On our right we skirt the islet of San Giacomo in Palude, with shaggy, stag-headed trees, choked by ivy. Here in the open the sky is one enormous dome without a drum; if it is a cloudy day, Shelley's beloved Euganean hills on the mainland will not be visible. Ahead the parochial church tower of Burano has come into view, leaning appreciably to the south, a prominent punctuation in this flat watery desert. The Madonna del Monte, next on the right, is a speck of an islet covered by a single ruinous barn, roofless. Now we slacken speed and chug down the wide canal of Mazzorbo, packed with unattractive little houses (of commuters to Mestre), each with a varnished and glazed front door, separated from its neighbour by a high wire fence. Santa Catarina stands at the end of the canal. A brief acceleration brings us to Torcello.

On disembarking we walk for a quarter of an hour along a towpath beside a stagnant green canal (it would be a compliment to call its opaque waters emerald) which emits a not disagreeable stench of drains and fish. On either bank are marshlands and some vineyards. How much of an island Torcello may be is difficult to determine except from the air. It is a series of mud flats between flowing tidal water and brackish streams. There seems to be only one bridge in the whole concatenation; and that is the Devil's Bridge linking the towpath to the opposite bank of our canal. It is of single span and made of wide but shallow steps. It is without balustrades like those shown in Carpaccio's paintings – a rare survival from Renaissance times, of which in Venice that over the Rio di San Felice is another example. After a handful of little Gothic houses the unpaved Piazzetta (it can hardly be termed Piazza) is reached. Once swarming with adders and buzzing with mosquitoes, it now echoes to the shrieks of school-children and other adolescents, the boys buying T-shirts and the girls nylon underclothes suspended from huge multi-coloured umbrella booths.

I began by stating that the year 452 witnessed the birth of Venice in that the people of Aquileia took to the lagoons on the destruction of their land-locked city. For nearly two centuries they had eked out a hand-to-mouth existence. Then, according to legend, the inhabitants of a less important mainland city than Aquileia, namely Altinum, situated some twelve miles south-east of Treviso and on the edge of the lagoons, were in 638 vouchsafed a divine warning by a voice from heaven to flee the advancing Lombards, again on the warpath. These people, called the Altinati, came to a very rapid decision. They were sick and tired of barbarian hordes. They would leave the mainland for good, and take whatever they could carry of most value – which were the treasures of the Christian faith: vessels, icons, saintly relics – with them. In a determined manner they moved to the edge of the Lagoon. In makeshift boats they cruised around before settling on a solid expanse of mud flat which they named Turricellum after the little tower of their native Altinum. Unlike the fluctuating refugees on the larger Rialto islands who, far from having settled, kept returning to the mainland the moment the invaders seemed quiescent, the Altinati stayed for good and turned Torcello into a prosperous community. Their reigning Bishop Paolo transferred the see of their old city to Torcello, where it remained under the metropolitan jurisdiction of the Patriarch of Grado. Torcello was for more than twelve and a half centuries the episcopate of the lagoons.

At first the new community flourished from the produce of her gardens, the trade of her wool and the multiplicity of her monasteries. She also profited from the Byzantine Emperor Leo III's preposterous proclamation of Iconoclasm in 727. In consequence many of the Ravenna masons and stone carvers fled to Torcello. The fact that the Exarchate of Ravenna, to which the lagoons professed loyalty, collapsed under siege to the Lombards twenty-four years later enabled the Altinati to continue employing these skilled workers without fear of retribution. But as Hugh Honour has observed, as Venice grew, so Torcello shrank. Gradually Torcello's trade was taken from her by the more centralized Rialto islands. Her enterprising inhabitants and merchants moved to Venice. She became a quarry from which arose the Venetian palaces whose builders looted the materials, stone and marble, even whole staircases and portals, of her ancient monuments. Nevertheless in the sixteenth century Torcello still had 20,000 inhabitants and twenty churches. By the eighteenth century her episcopal see was transferred to Burano; and Torcello was virtually abandoned. By the nineteenth century she was a wilderness, her few remaining citizens ravaged by malaria. Her villas, palaces, schools, monasteries and churches, having been dismantled and ransacked, were finally levelled to the ground, with the exception of the surviving cathedral and campanile, St Fosca's hardly less marvellous church, the picturesque fourteenth-century Palazzetto, once the seat of the Council, the Palazzo dell'Archivio and some nondescript cottages, which form a solitary group round the Piazzetta.

I know nothing [wrote A. W. Lindsay in 1847] in its way like Torcello; it is a scene *sui generis* for simplicity and solitude – and yet not melancholy, for they are not the ruins of fallen greatness; the emotions excited are akin rather to those one experiences in visiting the source of some mighty river, or gazing at the portrait of a hero in his childhood.

Torcello had become a detached retreat where a few inhabitants led pastoral lives tending their vines and growing enough vegetables and produce for their own needs amidst the ruins of a community whose fortunes and fame were but memories of a vanished past. She was a warning of what her own foster-child Venice might one day become. She was no more than a day's excursion (there was no accommodation for a prolonged visit), from the congested city for historians, archaeologists, poets and those in search of ancient

architecture and an abandoned landscape in splendid isolation and sweet tranquillity. John Ruskin, having spent a whole winter in Venice, wrote to his father on 24 May 1852 that

> there never was a place on which season made so much difference. The fields and vineyards in winter are lost among the marshy land – all trampled into mud – but now, they are separated from the canals which encircle the little island by hedges or briar and honeysuckle and hawthorn – and the vineyards are in young leaf – and in the little *piazza* of the ancient city – round its flagstaff they are mowing their hay – and it lies in fragrant heaps about the bases of the pillars of the cathedral – and all the peasantry look happy – and even healthy, the spring sunshine making their faces ruddy – they sing everywhere as they go . . .

Because the foundation of the cathedral at Torcello antedated that of St Mark's, nineteenth-century scholars were inclined to believe that the whole building dated from 639, which a stone tablet (still in the presbytery) records as the year of its consecration and dedication to Our Lady of the Assumption, while giving the names of the bishop and exarch responsible. In fact the original cathedral was much modified in 864 and almost totally reconstructed in 1008 on the basilican plan of nave and two aisles, each with apse, the nave apse probably being the only part now left standing of the seventh century. The baptistery of omega shape, built a few paces in front of the west entrance and now entirely ruinous but for two apsidal appendices, likewise dates from 639. As for the cathedral, it is the largest monument of the lagoons in the Byzantine style derived from Ravenna.

The façade is of plain brick. Its verticality is stressed by six blind arches over recessed panels running from ground almost to roof line, and pierced by random openings. The impressive elongation of the arcading is interrupted by a ninth-century portico and an ambulatory of the fourteenth to the fifteenth centuries, connecting cathedral to baptistery and Santa Fosca. The roof is supported by the surviving scrap of baptistery wall and a row of antique columns cut down to size. A rare feature is

22

the heavy shutters and hinges of stone to the windows of the south aisle. Ruskin saw this building 'as expressive at once of the deep sorrow and the sacred courage of the men who had no home left them upon earth, but who looked for one to come, of men "persecuted but not forsaken, cast down but not destroyed"'. In expressing this sentiment Ruskin was either forgetful or else unaware of the building's date, some four hundred years after the Altinati had fled once and for all the persecution of the Lombards. He was so impressed by the cathedral that 'I would rather fix the mind of the reader on this general character than on the separate details, however interesting, of the architecture itself'.

Whatever exactly he did mean, Ruskin was not unique in being deeply moved on entering by the south door, which is approached from the returning ambulatory. In spite of the succession of restorations, some injudicious, to which both exterior and interior have been submitted, the interior strikes you forcibly with its primitive simplicity combined with richness, its purity and holiness, as well as its luminosity. Ruskin attributed this almost numinous ethos to 'the men of sorrow's' desire for light and hatred of the darkness into which cruel circumstances had driven them. He bitterly deplored the removal to the Accademia gallery of Tintoretto's *Madonna and the Faithful* which he deemed the 'purest work' of the artist's heart 'and fairest of his faculty'. He did not believe that the great walls of unrelieved brick had ever, with the exception of course of the west wall, been covered with mosaic or fresco.

The north wall is indeed totally devoid of windows, having been intended to shield the congregations from the icy mountain blasts on this exposed quarter of the Adriatic. Only the south wall has clerestory windows which admit sunlight through small circular panes. The high roof of the nave is constructed of plain beams renewed during the Austrian occupation of Venice at the beginning of the last century. It is sustained by eighteen shiny grey columns of Greek marble like moiré silk (as Hugh Honour observes), with Corinthian capitals of an unorthodox sort. All these columns date from the eleventh century, with the exception of the second and third on the south side, which belong to the sixth. Ruskin, in his unshakeable conviction that the medieval Gothic was an improvement on the ancient Classical, ranked these capitals among the best he had ever seen. The naturalistic acanthus leaf of the upper range and the sharply cut vine foliage of the lower revealed clearly to him the enthusiasm, love of life and implicit faith of the medieval artisans. The Gothic sculptors had, in contrast to the old pagan masons, demonstrated the individual's respect for his craft and for the glorification of his God. The stalwart wooden tie-beams, which rest on the capitals to support the arches and indeed the whole body of the church against collapse in the event of earthquakes, provide a horizontal emphasis repeated in the iconastasis and rood screen of the chancel. Thick iron bands were at some time found necessary to ring the north columns of the sanctuary.

The iconastasis, signifying in Greek Orthodox churches the screen separating congregation from sanctuary behind which the clergy operated in strict seclusion, consists here of a transitional contrivance through which the laity can perfectly well observe the clergy and choristers in what is more a choir than a sanctuary. Raised two steps above the nave, six small columns carry a gallery composed of wooden panels on which are painted in glowing colours the Madonna flanked by the Apostles. It dates from the fifteenth century. Above the panels one of the wooden ties acts as a rood beam, carrying a large wooden crucifix. Between the outer columns of the iconastasis two pairs of panels (called *plutei*) in carved marble separate nave from choir. These exquisite examples of eleventh-century Byzantine sculpture depict animals and birds in relief. On the outer panels two lions sit amongst foliage like rather surprised professors. Their expressions are very benign; as unlike the emblems of strength as may be. On the inner *plutei* a pair of peacocks, symbolizing the Resurrection and the new life to be acquired by baptism, stretch their long necks to peck at grapes in a bowl. The north and south *plutei* of the choir, being unadorned, are so translucent that the sunlight shines through them. Attached to the iconastasis but within the nave, a pulpit (*ambone*) is composed of scraps of marble brought from the

mainland. It is reached by steps ruthlessly cut by the architect
to the size he needed from sections of antique entablatures and
reliefs, not set upright but laid sideways and even upside-down.
The projecting lectern is hollowed in a shallow curve so that the
preacher's missal or holy book may remain open at the required
page when laid upon it. Ruskin praised the rough-and-
readiness of the pulpit for not distracting the attention of the
congregation from what the preacher might be saying.

Within the choir are remnants of wooden stalls of intarsia
work by no means remarkable if we compare them with other
stalls in Venice, notably those in the Frari church. The existing
altar table is a wretched affair, reconstructed during the
restorations of 1929 from little broken columns. These columns
had been discarded when Baldassare Longhena erected a
Baroque high altar and ciborium on which flighty angels poised
themselves in rope-balancing attitudes. The year 1929 witnessed a good deal of de-baroquizing as well as the removal of
Tintoretto's painting. Under the existing altar table the
remains of San Elidoro, the first bishop of Altinum, are
enclosed within a Roman sarcophagus of the second to third
century.

Behind the table and within the great central apse are ranged
six rows of seats for the presbyters. Through the middle of them
steps rise steeply to the bishop's throne. Seats and steps have
been recently renovated in gaunt brick. The original marble
throne has gone. Did the so-called 'Throne of Attila' in the
Piazzetta once occupy this position and serve the bishop's
purpose? Too much scraping has taken place in this area and
the thin marble wall-facing within the apse is a modern
replacement. Until lately traces of ninth-century painting of
feigned drapery were visible. Ruskin approved of the eastern
extremity of the cathedral not being enclosed for exclusive
priestly functions, but remaining what he called 'a simple and
stern semi-circular recess' in which bishop and presbyters
might share with the people their devotions.

What gives this pre-eminently sacred building a supreme
distinction is the pavement and the mosaics. The spacious floor
is wholly marbled like a gigantic carpet in conventional

geometrical patterns – multicoloured *tesserae* of minute squares and ellipses within large panels bordered with fragments of the same grey marble of the nave columns. Nothing in nave or aisles disturbs the uniform carpet save the recumbent effigy in high relief of Bishop Paolo d'Altino who transferred the see from Altinum to Torcello. His curry-coloured figure, dating from the fifteenth century and much worn, is framed within a border of red Verona marble. The very ordinary pews are incidentally not fixtures and can easily be removed.

William Beckford made a pilgrimage to Torcello in August 1780. Having walked over crumbling bricks and cement to the Cathedral he was particularly struck by the pavement and mosaics.

> Nothing can be more fantastic [he wrote] than the ornaments of this structure, formed from the ruins of the Pagan temples of Altina, and incrusted with gilt mosaic, like that which covers our Edward the Confessor's tomb [in Westminster Abbey]. The pavement, composed of various precious marbles, is richer and more beautiful than one could have expected, in a place where every other object savours of the grossest barbarism.

Beckford was then twenty years old and, like most cognoscenti of his time, still under the spell of the Augustan Classical, and had not yet sampled Gothic tastes. He observed the 'semicircular niche with seats like a diminutive amphitheatre; above quaint forms of the Apostles in red, blue, green. A marble chair [the bishop's], then still in place'. He studied too what he called the fount for holy water (*l'aquasantiere*) which still stands to the right of the west entrance, and pronounced 'the horned imps' which cling to its sides 'devilish', which they are, if not 'more Egyptian than any ever beheld'. Certainly these horrid little caryatids, some upside-down, resemble magnified tadpoles or human embryos. Further comments by Beckford were interrupted by the smell of dinner preparing for his party in a neighbouring convent. While they ate their improvised meal to the sound of music the nuns watched sadly and enviously through their grilles. But they bore no resentment or grudge. The Mother Superior blessed them when they left, invoking upon them a happy issue out of their profane joys.

The mosaics are what most visitors to Torcello seek as first priority. Unquestionably the great west wall depicting *The Last Judgement* from floor to ceiling is a stupendous affair in conception and execution. Yet like most massive pictures crammed with detail by no matter what eminent artist – Michelangelo's Sistine Chapel fresco comes within this category – it is not wholly satisfying. Although the Torcello *Last Judgement* fresco is at least visible and its parts can be picked out clearly through binoculars owing to the adequate light which is totally deficient in, say, St Mark's, yet no subject on this scale can be taken in as a whole by the naked eye. It is true that, unlike Michelangelo's *Last Judgement* which is painted as one scene, the Torcello mosaic, executed during the twelfth and thirteenth centuries, is divided into six separate zones – *Christ Crucified between St John the Evangelist and the Virgin* (under the rafters), *Christ in Judgement, Christ in Glory, Christ's Descent into Limbo, The Saved,* and *The Damned,* who notwithstanding the eternal flames confronting them, wear provoking expressions of complacency. In spite of repeated renovations, this tapestry of Christ's mercy offered to his church and promise of his second coming is a technical masterpiece. It sheds a kaleidoscopic glow of colours from a cold background. There survive few Christian artefacts in narrative form better calculated to fill simple and illiterate viewers with hope or despondency.

James Morris sees in the full-length figure of the *Madonna Teotòca* (the Mother of God) bearing the Child in her arms in the east central apse, the noblest memorial in the Lagoon. This mosaic is of indeterminate date. Although the rigid, hieratic pose of the Lady of Sorrows is Byzantine, deriving from the seventh century, the exposition here probably belongs to the late twelfth or early thirteenth century. With anguish and tear – the size of a golf ball – on cheek, she gazes from a heaven of pale gold over the iconastasis at the congregation in the nave with a sternness calculated to make her earthly children quail rather than adore. Below her are ranged the Apostles, in the words of Henry James, 'against their dead gold backgrounds as stiffly as grenadiers presenting arms – intensely personal sentinels of a personal Deity. Their stony stare seems to wait forever vainly for some visible revival of primitive orthodoxy.'

More appealing to me is the twelfth-century mosaic in the lesser apse of the south aisle, depicting Christ enthroned between the Archangels Gabriel and Michael. With his right hand raised in blessing and his left clutching the holy scriptures he sits firmly on a Byzantine cushion, the upturning ends of which indicate the weight of the body upon the centre. But the glory of this composition is the vault in front of the holy apotheosis. Four angels, two of them with their feet on the globe, uphold with raised arms a circular shield of the Mystic Lamb. The conception is almost Baroque in movement and freedom from the customary Byzantine immobility. In fact it is largely copied from the vault of the archiepiscopal chapel at San Vitale in Ravenna which dates from the fifth to sixth centuries.

Reached from the cathedral by the ambulatory is the little eleventh to twelfth-century church of Santa Fosca, an obscure saint. This church has always been played down by the guidebooks; and yet it is one of the most harmoniously proportioned churches in the Lagoon. In conception it is oriental; in execution western. The ambulatory, which does not entirely encompass it, consists of five sides of an octagon, leaving the apsed east end of the church exposed. The alternate sides of the ambulatory have highly stilted arches on carved Byzantine columns, with four openings to the longer and three to the shorter sides. The church itself is a Greek cross with truncated arms. It is crowned by an elaborate cornice in terracotta. The plan of the interior – all of brick – is a circle within a quadrangle. A large dome, never completed, was intended to rest on the squinches. The squinches are supported by double-arched piers and coupled columns of grey marble. The apsed presbytery is semi-domed. Its narrow aisles are likewise apsed. Undecorated and full of light, Santa Fosca is a rare specimen of a Romanesque church begun by Greek workmen who deserted the job, leaving it to be completed by Venetians.

The eleventh-century campanile stands detached a few yards from the east end of the cathedral. The arrangement was deliberate in order to afford refuge to clergy and sacred treasures in the event of armed attack from the ubiquitous barbarians. Not divided into zones like the Lombard, nor round like the Ravennese, it is typical of the Venetian campanili. The square shaft of brick with vertical recessions, running from top to bottom, is pierced at one angle by little windows placed one above another to light the staircase. The bell-chamber has on each side four openings, their arched heads resting on little marble columns.

Ruskin's famous lines in which he advises the tourist to climb the campanile at twilight to enjoy the view has been extensively and rightly quoted as one of the purplest of his prose passages.

> Far as the eye can reach, a waste of wild sea moor, of a lurid ashen grey; not like our northern moors with their jet-black pools and purple heath, but lifeless, the colour of sackcloth, with the corrupted sea-water soaking through the roots of its acrid weeds, and gleaming hither and thither through its snaky channels. No gathering of fantastic mists, nor coursing of clouds across it; but melancholy clearness of space in the warm sunset, oppressive, reaching to the horizon of its level gloom. To the very horizon, on the north-east; but, to the north and west, there is a blue line of higher land along the border of it, and above this, but further back, a misty band of mountains, touched with snow. To the east, the paleness and roar of the Adriatic, louder at momentary intervals as the surf breaks on the bars of the sand; to the south, the widening branches of the calm lagoon, alternately purple and pale green, as they reflect the evening clouds or twilight sky. . .
>
> Then look further to the south. Beyond the widening branches of the Lagoon, and rising out of the bright lake into which they gather, there are a multitude of towers, dark, and scattered among square-set shapes of clustered palaces, a long and irregular line fretting the southern sky.
>
> Mother and daughter, you behold them both in their widowhood – Torcello and Venice.

Alas, access is no longer granted to the tourist, only to the privileged sacristan or guardian of the campanile, who is bound occasionally to ascend and possibly enjoy what, with but little change, the great apostle of the Gothic so much admired.

Looking down immediately below him Ruskin's eye took in the cattle feeding upon the site of the almost deserted city of the Altinati: 'The mower's scythe swept this day at dawn over the chief street of the city that they built, and the swathes of soft grass are now sending up their scent into the night air, the only incense that fills the temple of their ancient worship.' The Piazzetta was, and is, hardly larger than an ordinary English farmyard, then enclosed on each side by broken palings and hedges of honeysuckle and briar. During the evening of my last visit it was, as I have already said, swarming with Italian school-children uttering raucous obscenities, rendering the air hideous with their competing transistors, and rushing into the cathedral where they jumped on the pews and photographed one another in the confessionals.

I decided to block my ears, avert my eyes and imagine that I was alone. Perhaps, I thought, if one chose a fine day in February one might recapture the tranquillity that reigned in Torcello when I first knew it. After all, Beckford, as we have seen, and even the Ruskins in their more restrained way made merry on Torcello. And why not? Effie wrote to her mother on 24 February 1850 that she and John, with friends, had a picnic there the previous day. From a cloth spread on the ground they ate cold fowls, Parmesan cheese, Italian bread, beef and cakes, washed down with Muscat and Champagne wines. While Effie and Charlotte, her special friend, looked for violets not yet out amid the dead leaves of yesteryear,

> John and Paulizza [an Austrian officer whom Effie rather fancied] were in the highest spirits and nothing could be merrier than the two. After dinner, to show us that the Champagne which they certainly did not take much of, had not gone into their heads, they ran races round the old buildings and so fast that one could hardly see them. Paulizza looked so funny with his sword jumping at every step and Blue spectacles on.

It is rather refreshing to know that an earnest and humourless art historian can sometimes throw care to the winds and behave like an ordinary mortal. We have to bear in mind however that the Beckford and Ruskin parties were probably the only people present and that for days before and after their visits no one may have gone there at all. Our misfortune is that too many people are herded onto Torcello who haven't a clue to the ineffable delights to be enjoyed by the initiated, for whom they merely make a hell out of a paradise.

ST MARK'S

1063–94

To write about St Mark's is to plumb the depths of unwisdom. For one who is not a specialist to hold forth about the authorship and dates of the sculpture, mosaics and other artefacts which embellish this magical building is to invite derision. In the first place, eminent men of letters and poets of every tongue have eulogized the building; and every scholar has speculated about the works of art as well as the architecture of St Mark's. In the second place, when we approach a building which is magical what do attributions and dates matter? The experts themselves have been known to get into deep water – by which I mean make fools of themselves – because, of the hundreds of artists who have worked on St Mark's, the Byzantine often copied the Greek, the Gothic the Byzantine, the Renaissance the Gothic, and the seventeenth-, eighteenth- and nineteenth-century Venetians imitated everybody. The medieval Venetians are known to have tampered with the Roman sculpture, and the mosaicists of every century since the tenth altered and faked the work of preceding centuries.

It should be remembered that Venice's patron saint was not originally St Mark. For several centuries the Greek San Todoro (or St Theodore) of Heraclea was the acknowledged protector of the Venetian populace. When the Republic became a great Mediterranean power in the ninth century, Todoro, whose status in the hierarchy of saints had always been undistinguished, was demoted on the grounds that he symbolized the dependence of Venice upon Byzantium. Nevertheless he was not irrevocably banished and was allowed to stand over his crocodile (the emblem of venom) on the column in front of the

Sansovino Library in the Piazzetta. In looking around for a more prestigious patron than poor Todoro the Venetians deemed no saint below the dignity of an Evangelist worthy of consideration. So by a chain of miraculous deductions and eventualities St Mark was adopted. Legend conveniently established his just claims. It was stated that during his lifetime the Evangelist, before being called to Rome by St Peter, founded the church at Aquileia where he even wrote his Gospel. And when one day his boat was driven by a high wind against a bank of the Rialto, an angel's voice was heard by the Apostle to exclaim, 'Peace be to thee, Mark; here shall thy body rest.' However for many years the saint's body contentedly rested in Alexandria, and looked like remaining there. This was unfortunate but there were ways of getting round the difficulty, by guile.

In 829 two patriotic Venetian merchants took the matter into their own hands, neither forewarning nor discussing the project with the doge lest he demur over their thoroughly immoral intentions or object, as he almost certainly would, to their ostensible trading with heathens. Having elicited through bribery the aid of two Greek monks, the merchants sailed to Alexandria, stole the corpse, and put the remains of some inferior saint in its place. The conspirators packed the Evangelist's body in a basket which they covered with pork, anathema to the Moslem Egyptians, and weighed anchor. On reaching Venice they received the delighted doge's pardon for the offence of trading with the heathen. After resting for a time in the Ducal Palace the body was interred in the church built for it. Its possession was used as an important weapon in Venice's struggle for ecclesiastical and political independence of Rome and Byzantium.

Just as St Peter is traditionally depicted by artists as an elderly man with grey hair and the keys of heaven, so St Mark is given in mosaics and Renaissance paintings the likeness of a burly man with square-shaped head, low brow, small eyes, and thick brown hair. With his determined jaw he resembles a benevolent bruiser.

The first church of St Mark was built by two brothers Partecipazii, successively doges, on a cruciform plan and finished in 832. It stood to the north of the chapel of San Isidore of the present cathedral and on the site of a church dedicated to the demoted San Todoro. What little decoration it had – for archaeologists claim that it had no marble, no colour and no mosaics – continued to be applied until 883. Nothing of the Partecipazii church is visible today. It did not survive long, and in 976 was destroyed by fire deliberately set by the citizens to the Ducal Palace in a rebellion against the oppressive Doge Pietro Candiano. Towards the close of the tenth century it was rebuilt, possibly in replica, on the same cruciform plan as the first by Doges Orseoli I and Orseoli II. This second church lasted an even shorter time than the first. It was pulled down and from 1063 onwards rebuilt. Doge Domenico Contarini felt impelled to raise a more magnificent building to the glory of St Mark and the Serene Republic. After all, St Mark's was not the cathedral church of Venice – that was the rub. It was the doge's personal chapel and remained so until 1807, nine years after the Republic had been obliterated by Napoleon. The cathedral was San Pietro di Castello, on an island at the eastern extremity of the city. The bishops of San Pietro were traditionally too subservient to the popes at Rome for the doges' liking. In fact doges nominated and invested, without the approval of the bishop of Castello or the patriarch of Ravenna, the highest ecclesiastic of St Mark's, who was called the primicerius (or chaplain). He was always selected from one of the leading Venetian families. He was subject to the doge solely, and even the Roman Curia tacitly recognized this, if it did not acknowledge his right to mitre, ring and staff. The office of primicerate lasted until 1810.

All the city's greatest celebrations took place at St Mark's. When a doge was elected the people came to St Mark's to acclaim him. In the church the doge worshipped in the grandeur of his dignity – ermine tippet, crimson shoes, and that astonishing golden cap (the *còrnu*) on his head. His private door from the Ducal Palace was through the Cappella San Clemente on the south side of the sanctuary. There he sat on a throne in the customary Eastern tradition as in Constantinople, and not elevated in a balcony. When he died his body was borne across the Piazza aloft to the central opening of the atrium so that the people might see it. Before the great door to the church within the atrium Pope Alexander III and the Emperor Frederick I (Barbarossa) were reconciled in 1177 through the medium of Doge Sebastiano Ziani, not before the Emperor submitted his neck as a footstool, exclaiming as he did so, '*Non tibi, sed Petro,*' and evoking from the victorious pontiff the rejoinder, '*Et Petro et mihi.*' A lozenge of porphyry marks the exact spot. In 1201 the first crusade was proclaimed from the pulpit. When the plot laid by Marino Faliero was revealed in 1355 and when the naval victory in the Dardanelles was celebrated in 1656, the doge headed a procession across the Piazza to the church. Nevertheless only a handful of eleventh-century doges were buried in St Mark's and they were confined to benefactors who had spent large sums on building and decorating it.

From 1063 to 1071, the year in which he died, Doge Contarini rebuilt and embellished the St Mark's we recognize. This long-reigning doge, by dint of the close alliance he forged with Byzantium through military support of, trade with and the marriage of his children into the imperial family, greatly raised the prosperity and prestige of Venice.

Doge Contarini's St Mark's is, unlike its predecessors, of Greek cross plan. It was specifically modelled on that of the church of the Holy Apostles (or Apostoleion) in Constantinople, which had been built by Justinian in the second quarter of the sixth century, and was destroyed in 1463. Transepts were added, the sanctuary was extended and the atrium was continued round the sides. These alterations were deliberate so that the building should fulfil the function of a martyrium, that is to say afford access from all sides to the devout assembling to pay homage to the Evangelist's shrine. The contrast with Torcello Cathedral on the basilican, or Latin cross plan, is very telling. Yet there were necessary differences between St Mark's and its Byzantine prototype, the Apostoleion. Unlike the Apostoleion the presbytery of St Mark's is raised to allow for a crypt, and is apsed to allow for a high altar which in the case of the Apostoleion was immediately under the central dome. St Mark's is not exclusively a martyrium. But, like the Apostoleion, it has five domes, of which the two over the transepts are smaller than the three over the main axis.

It is noteworthy that by the second half of the eleventh century Venice had become rich enough, politically important enough and had at her service the technical knowledge and equipment to approximate St Mark's to the Apostoleion. This was not the case in the ninth and tenth centuries when the first and second St Mark's were built. The main technical innovation of the third church was the grand brick vaulting in place of the wooden roofs of the two earlier churches. Yet the fact that the third church was built so urgently suggests that the second had not been wholly demolished. Decorative work in the way of marble and mosaic was well in hand at the end of the eleventh century. A close approximation to St Mark's – and as it were its progeny, for it dates from *circa* 1120 – is the church of St Front at Périgueux in the Dordogne, a product of Byzantine influence carried west along the trade routes by Venetian merchants. In plan and setting of cupolas the French church is identical to the parent, though lacking mosaics, the essential ingredient of Byzantine ecclesiastical architecture, so that the interior is bare and gaunt by comparison.

With the capture of Constantinople in 1204 and the foundation of the Venetian empire in the Levant, Venice was flooded with artists and works of art from Byzantium. Having destroyed the Greek capital she looted it. Treasures, not only gold and silver vessels studded with gems but marble reliefs, columns and painted icons, were imported briskly from the East for some fifty years. St Mark's was embellished with, amongst other things, the three pulpits, the ciborium of the high altar, harbouring the miracle-working crucifix and the icon of the Nikopeia, all brought from Constantinople.

At first the Venetians had no creative ideas of their own, but by 1250 the fascination of looted treasure waned. By now Venice was a world power. Venetian artists and craftsmen, deeply influenced by what for half a century they had been bringing from Byzantium, set about evolving, notably in sculpture, works of art of their own inspiration. The Venetian proto-Renaissance was in full swing. But in the third quarter of the thirteenth century this creative period slackened owing to the re-establishment of the Greeks in Byzantium. A new wave of Byzantine influence washed over Venice. Furthermore, Venice was now faced with a new menace from the West in the shape of the powerful maritime republic of Genoa. The struggle against this formidable rival dragged on until 1380, when Venice's defeat of Genoa left her undisputed mistress of the Mediterranean as well as the Adriatic. During her contacts with Genoa she necessarily fell under the influence of the Romanesque and Gothic.

In the early Middle Ages it was considered indispensable for a metropolitan church of the repute of St Mark's to contain as many holy relics as possible. It was a matter of prestige, like a wireless aerial in England to pretentious households in the 1930s and a swimming pool in the 1950s. To contain part of, if not the whole anatomy of the saint to whom the church was dedicated was not merely indispensable; it was absolutely *de rigueur*.

Now an unfortunate thing happened during Doge Contarini's remodelling of St Mark's between 1063 and 1071. The Evangelist's body, acquired at such cost and by such dubious means, and placed with the utmost solemnity in the first St Mark's in 836, was lost. Its whereabouts had been confided to the Doge and the Primicerius, and no one else. During the upheaval of the rebuilding Doge Domenico Contarini and the Primicerius, who had deposited the remains in a safe place, both died. When the day arrived for the re-dedication of the new edifice the body was nowhere to be found. Three days of fasting and intensive prayer were ordained. Then miraculously a surviving pillar of the previous church opened of its own accord, disclosing the sarcophagus of the saint, his body uncorrupted. Certain witnesses even maintained that a beckoning hand was drawing their attention to his plight; and that in gratitude for his release the Evangelist allowed a member of the noble Dolfin family to remove a gold ring from his finger. The legend can be traced back to thirteenth century.

During the course of time other relics, some no less sacred than the Evangelist's errant corpse, accrued. They were housed in the treasury. Among the most cherished were a phial containing drops of the Sacred Blood of Jesus Christ, a piece of the ubiquitous True Cross, a nail therefrom, a thorn from the Sacred Crown, an arm of St George, a fragment of the skull of St John the Baptist, and an arm of St Pantaleon. Numerous relics perished in a fire of 1230–31, but most of those listed above were much admired by the English visitor Fynes Moryson during his itinerary of 1594, in addition to others which may within the last four hundred years have been dispersed. The clergy today are shy of parading and even discussing these things. The additional relics which Moryson observed were a piece of the bone of St Philip, a piece of the cheekbone and four teeth of St Biagius; some of the hair of the Virgin Mary; the tip of one of St Luke's fingers; a rib of St Peter; and also the rock struck by Moses, still exuding water. The slightly incredulous Fynes made a note of the exculpatory couplet incised above the altar of St Clement:

> Nam Deus est quod Imago docet, sed non Deus ipse
> Hanc videas, sed mente colas quod cernis in ipso.

Many of these precious relics, together with the immense treasure accumulated over the centuries, were either jettisoned, purloined or sold by Napoleon's orders on the fall of the Republic in 1797. Eight persons, appointed to the task of destruction, 'worked with vandalistic fury for a few days'.* Gold and silver vessels were melted down, including the ducal crown, the twelve gold corselets and lesser crowns. The Pala d'Oro was saved only by certain officials claiming that it was not made of valuable metals. On 3 January 1802 some precious books were returned to the treasury. But with the coming of the French a second time the collection was ransacked again and mostly auctioned. 'The sold jewels were the diamonds, 700 carat pearls, a dozen big heavy sapphires amounting to 1400 carats, 2269 carat emeralds, four big 330 carat amethysts, fourteen rubies and all the *balassi* (a sort of ruby), weighing altogether 10514 carats.'†

In 1814 Venice fell to the Austrians. Still more treasures were dispersed at auction in 1819. Even so, many survive, including

---

*G. Musolini, *The Basilica of St Mark in Venice*, 1955.
†A. Pasini, *Il Tesoro di San Marco in Venezia*, 1885–6.

the reliquary containing the Precious Blood. The best presumably are not displayed for when you pay to enter the treasury today you will not be rewarded by very spectacular exhibits. The entrance portal itself is worth all the present contents put together. But how few passing through it look up at the wonderful inflected arch, a sort of double ogee, almost Moorish in composition, of the thirteenth century. Between two adoring angels in mosaic the lunette holds a fourteenth-century statuette, *Ecce Homo*.

The great west façade of St Mark's seen from the Piazza is so famous that any description must be otiose. Over a hundred years ago Henry James wrote, 'I must not, however, speak of St. Mark's as if I had the pretension of giving a description of it, or as if the reader desired one. The reader has been too well served already. It is surely the best-described building in the world.' How right he was. And Max Beerbohm too, in recording that he 'should not envy the soul of one who at first sight of such strange loveliness found anything to say'. Whereupon he promptly said it, and very much to the point too. To him the whole church had less the effect of a building than a garden, 'an Eastern garden that had by some Christian miracle petrified just when the flowers were fading, so that its beauty should last forever to the Glory of Christ and of St. Mark.' 'And observe', Max added, 'that Mahommed had walked there, and his spirit walks there yet.'

To be prosaic, one's first impression, particularly if that impression was implanted in the mind during one's early romantic youth, of this fairy-like structure, is in recollection doubtless the true and lasting picture of St Mark's façade. The glowing gold and white, gold and grey vision has been known, literally, to take the breath away and reduce the viewer to a state almost of fainting, and sometimes bordering on hysteria. 'That strange cathedral!' Richard Monckton Milnes exclaimed in the 1830s,

> exquisitely strange –
> That front, on whose bright varied tints the eye
> Rests as of gems – those arches, whose high range

Gives its rich-broidered border to the sky –
Those ever prancing steeds!

Breathlessly his verse ends in the reproach of a friend to whom
the poem was addressed for not conceding quite the same
enthusiasm as his own. Actually the façade of St Mark's is not
remarkable for a 'high range'. It is not vertical. It is a horizontal
structure, suitably punctuated by the three domes visible when
confronted full face. Its horizontality is emphasized by the
strong, straight lines of the imposts of the two orders which
support the arches and the gallery balustrade. It is further
stressed by the elongation of the atrium, the end bays being left
open so as to reveal the continuation of the walk along the side
façades.

St Mark's cannot be confronted full face until one is close to
it, owing to the Piazza being an imperfect rectangle and tilted,
so to speak, to the south. This means that on approaching it
one does not get a full view until about half way along the
Procuratie Vecchie (on the north side). This condition may
even be to one's advantage, for one's first view of St Mark's is
of a building at an angle in its own eccentric and appealing
stance.

Far the best interpretation of the astonishing façade is
Gentile Bellini's painting done five hundred years ago. And of
how many old buildings in the modern world can such a thing
be said? St Mark's has altered in very few respects since then
albeit Bellini saw it in the pristine splendour of its gold-
crocketed crestings and snow-white pinnacles, tumbling over
the star-spangled blue background to the winged lion; all so
newly imposed. For the decorative details of the façade coeval
with the building, the friezes, the scrolls, the interlacings of
foliage and the mysterious beasts are visible in what is surely
the earliest painting of the façade. The façade is also illustrated, though less minutely, in the even earlier mosaic head
of the left portal, called the Porta Sant'Alippio. The raised
cupolas and the four horses are shown in this mosaic of 1267.
The body of St Mark in his bier is seen carried by the
Primicerius and the Patriarch into the church, though both

these worthies are made to face the spectator outwards. It is a very bold illustration in colouring; a step away from the Byzantine.

The west façade conforms to a symmetrical pattern down to the row of six reliefs in the spandrels between the opening arches, as shown in the Sant'Alippio mosaic. These reliefs are not to be read as a sequence, and are in fact a mingling of mythological and Christian subjects. *Hercules with the boar* by a Greek sculptor of the thirteenth century and taken from an antique statue, is duplicated. The second *Hercules* is a Venetian paraphrase of the Byzantine first. *St Demetrius* and *St George* bear the same relationship. St George is actually a dull and flat though minute copy of the Byzantine St Demetrius. The *Madonna Orant*, somewhat surprisingly not given a central stance, is by a Venetian sculptor superior to him of the two copies already mentioned. This duplicating of Byzantine models in the thirteenth century marked the emergence of the Venetian school of sculpture. Their work was prevented from lapsing into mere convention by the Romanesque influences introduced to Venice from the West.

And what of the four preposterously placed horses prancing in front of the great black window? Their history has been peripatetic. They were intended by their ancient Greek creator of the fourth to third century BC for an Athenian *quadriga*. They are said to have crowned a triumphal arch for Nero and then Trajan in Rome. But they were not destined to remain long in the imperial city. With the break-up of the empire in the West they were transported to the island of Chios, and thence to Constantinople. There Doge Enrico Dandalo found them on the towers of the Hippodrome, and on the destruction of the Eastern capital, brought them with other loot to Venice.

At first they adorned the Arsenal. About 1250 they were put in their present position, symbols of victory, where they are shown in the Sant'Alippio mosaic, as we have just remarked, only a few years later. The arch-barbarian Napoleon removed them to Paris in 1798, setting them in front of the Tuileries Palace, then in 1805 on the triumphal arch of the Carousel. They were returned to Venice in 1815 where Byron saw them back in place, each on its pedestal in 1818:

Before St. Mark still glow his Steeds of brass,
Their gilded collars glittering in the sun.

And although they no more belong to St Mark than to Chios, to
the Christian church than to the pagan island, yet one prays
they may never again be exiled overseas.

Unfortunately what we see today are replicas made by Art
Battaglia, Milan, in 1980. The green bronze stallions have
turned to chestnut fibreglass. The glorious originals have had
to be transferred to a perfectly satisfying stable behind the
façade. There, cleaned and restored from the condition to
which the pollution from Mestre was rapidly reducing them,
they can be examined at close quarters. Unbridled, but
wearing collars, the stallions, every vein visible, their manes cut
like combs with occasional breaks in the hair, are beautifully
shown and lit. Proudly they stand in pairs, their arched necks
and noble heads inclined almost affectionately one to the other,
pristine, greeny grey and gold – Grecian gold – the scratches on
their breasts and flanks still a memory of the caster's work.
Surely they are the best bred horses in the whole world. And
could the most indifferent to horseflesh fail to admire them?
Max Beerbohm remarked that they made him feel very small,
very common. This they must do to everyone of humility. At
the same time they make one admire and love them very much
indeed.

Of the two orders of shafts which compose the five great
openings of the renowned west façade all are of porphyry,
alabaster, *verde antico* and other rare marbles brought as spoils
from Constantinople. The observant Coryate was quick to
notice that several of 'these goodly pillars', notably those
brought from Pontius Pilate's house in Jerusalem, were so
cracked and broken that no weight could be put on them. They
are used as adornments and support virtually nothing. They
are all in the round, of unequal measurements with spaces
between them and the walls. Adrian Stokes discovered in the
cavernous portals a singularity and independence of each unit.
In the dark channels between the unequal columns he detected
a reflection of the black waterways in the heart of old Venice.

The central porch is what Otto Demus terms 'a symbiosis of various elements which makes the Venetian'. He advises us that the sculpture must be read from the innermost soffit to the outer, that is to say, 'moving from the general to the particular, from the spiritual to the secular, and from the abstract to the concrete', if we are to interpret correctly the stories the sculptors meant to tell. For example,

> The soffit of the innermost arch shows symbolic figures, mostly animals, fighting or acting as the protagonists of fables; on the face of the arch the actors of the symbolic scenes are human beings, both children and adults. In the next arch the symbols have been replaced by allegories; the soffit shows allegorical figures of the Months; the front, personifications of the Virtues.

These Virtues were, as it happens, copied from figures on the mosaics of the central cupola inside the church. The reliefs of thickly concentrated figures on the soffit of the second arch are most important in that they represent in allegorical terms the evolution of time from chaos to order as understood by the Christian Logos.

Finally, the last arch of the central porch displays the Venetian trades of everyday life. As Demus says, 'these genre scenes of human activities are not at all allegorized or generalized images'. This arch contains the most accomplished sculpture of the series. The whole cycle of handicrafts by men and women in the lagoons is faithfully represented. A young man wearing a pointed hood digs with a long spade. Observe the dreamy look as he carries on with his pedestrian task. A boy catches limed birds. His expression is of intense concentration. Below him a man astraddle a deer thrusts a knife into the poor beast's upturned head. Another man carries the branch of a tree over his shoulder. An old man with a fish round his neck washes his feet in a flowing stream. On the soffit of the third arch the very personalized figure of another old man with crutches, biting the fingers of his right hand, is thought to be the architect of the church in a state of shame over his presumption in boasting that he could have built another more beautiful than St Mark's. I know no Gothic images more true to daily life, more detailed, more down to earth or more poetic than these figures. The nameless sculptor of these carvings, dated *circa* 1250, is known as The Master of the Calendar Cycle. The beautiful columns that support the ciborium of the high altar, densely carved with small figures in relief, are likewise his.

'The series of prophets on the front of the arch, with Christ in the apex is prefixed to this entire system as a kind of titlepage', Demus concludes. They make an adequate framework for the treasures within but in themselves are stiff and conventional. Over all in the lunette of the doorway the central theme of the whole conception is the mosaic of *The Last Judgement*, restored it is true in 1838, but nevertheless preserving its original outline.

The fourteenth and fifteenth centuries saw the façade enriched with new windows, cornices and sculpture after the upper storey had blossomed into wave-like crests, canopies and statues. From 1500 onwards no changes took place, with the exception of the mosaics. Apart from those in the lunette of the Sant'Alippo portal, the mosaics of the other portals are unashamedly seventeenth-, eighteenth- and nineteenth-century restorations or replacements. These substitutes have been unanimously deplored since Henry James complained that, 'today that admirable harmony of faded mosaic and marble, which to the eye of the traveller . . . filled all the farther end [of the Piazza] with a sort of dazzling silvery presence – today this lovely vision is in a way to be completely reformed and, indeed, well-nigh abolished.'

The last act of vandalism took place in 1884; and deplorable it undoubtedly was. Yet, at the risk of seeming insensitive, I am grateful that the original mosaics were at least replaced. Within the dark shadowed caverns where they stand, their indifference as works of art is anyway hard to distinguish and after a century the general picture has, through time's kindly weathering, in some respect brought back the 'dazzling silvery presence' to which the famous novelist referred. More noticeable and more deplorable in my judgement are the crude patches of new material on the north and south façades of St Mark's to which James referred as having 'the effect of a monstrous malady rather than of a restoration to health. They look like blotches of red and white paint and dishonourable smears of chalk on the cheeks of a noble matron', only a slight exaggeration of the crude re-marbling of both façades.

Let it not be supposed that the recurrent restorations of St Mark's were not essential. It is the manner of carrying them out that was so often reprehensible. Shifting foundations, faulty brick and other materials, floods and fires caused repeated damage to the fabric. Sansovino, who held the post of Proto, which means architect to the church, for over forty years, was obliged to do an immense amount of restoration during the sixteenth century. He supported the foundations. He inserted tie-beams within. He erected buttresses, bound the church with heavy bands of iron and the collapsing domes with hoops. In the seventeenth century Baldassare Longhena was Proto for fifty years. He restored the west façade, the north dome and the roof over the sacristy. He enlarged the five small windows of the arch above the altar of the Madonna and those of the tympanum wall above the outer door of the baptistery.

Repairs continued throughout the eighteenth century, not always commendably. More chains round the domes were found necessary. Ruskin considered the replacement of the old mosaic over the central portal in 1838 an abomination; but actually it is inoffensive. The 1850s witnessed an unfortunate campaign of deliberate restoration for its own sake. The north and south lateral façades were virtually renewed. Everything crooked was straightened. Columns and capitals were scraped; old marble slabs were replaced by new ones, and the floor of the left aisle was levelled by the firm of Salviati. A. E. Street, in the biography of his father, the well-known architect G. E. Street, affirmed that his father was largely responsible for persuading the authorities to leave the rest of the interior pavement alone. He even went so far as to convince them that the undulations had been intentional on the part of the builders to reflect the waves of the sea. Ruskin raved and raged and invoked the protests of the Society for the Protection of Ancient Buildings – not, oddly, without effect. Still in the 1890s injudicious restoration of interior walls continued and old mosaics were replaced by new. With the appointment of Ferdinando Forlati as Proto in 1948 a happier phase of restitution with the most modern and yet conservative methods was ushered in.

The south façade had fared very badly. Notwithstanding almost total restoration one's eyes are ravished by the beauty of the upper stage behind the balustrading: the crockets of the gables like wild white breakers along the sea shore, the enchanting tiered canopies from the coronals of which, faintly touched with gold, rise spirelets so fragile that one almost fears the waves just referred to, or the wing of a careless pigeon, may smash them to smithereens. And whose is the saintly figure standing on the apex of the second, and incidentally smaller, gable? Justice or Strength? Surely Gentleness, for her face is angelic and she comforts a lamb which, standing on its hind legs on the perilous apex, reaches to receive a stroke or pat. Other detail on this upper range is there to enchant, namely the *Virgin Orant*, a thirteenth-century Byzantine mosaic within a central niche head. Every evening two lamps (it must be admitted that today they are electrified) have been lit in expiation of the unjust execution of a baker's boy for a murder he never committed.

And before leaving this front can one fail to be mystified by the two pairs of porphyry brethren with their broken noses, called the Tetrarchs, embracing one another while the left hand of each firmly grasps a sword hilt? How sinister they are. And one shudders on passing the porphyry stone at the far corner, described by Coryate as 'of a pretty large compass, even as much as a man can clasp at twice with both his arms'. One can visualize Coryate, the most meticulous of sightseers, who felt obliged to prove every point he recorded by suiting actions to words. 'On this stone are laid for the space of three days and three nights, the heads of all such' as were enemies to the state – no doubt the poor baker's boy's amongst them. 'The smell of them doth breed a very offensive and contagious annoyance.'

Today the irregular north front overlooking the Piazzetta dei Leoncini does not in the least resemble the original Contarini front, which was regular. The nineteenth century saw to that. Nevertheless it is still liberally embellished with sculptural fragments, mostly looted from the East and moved here from the interior of the church in subsequent centuries. For instance *The Ascension of Alexander the Great to Heaven* is a Byzantine relief of the tenth century. Note in the third arcade the rectangular panel of the *Hetoismasia* (seventh century), a throne crested with a medallion of the Lamb, flanked by a dozen other lambs and two palm trees; also two roundels of a peacock pecking a rabbit's head, and a winged lion standing upon a hind. These display early Christian symbolism.

The four arched recesses under the balustrading of the north side are of course part of that projection from the church which forms the atrium. The atrium was from the first regarded, not as part of the church, but as a passage where it was legitimate for the public to amble, protected from the winter rain and the summer sun. In the eighteenth century it was often a rendez-vous for dalliance; and sometimes a refuge from the vile stench of human bodies inside the church. Beckford, who was very pernickety, was so overcome that he ran up the campanile in order to be restored by draughts of fresh air from the Adriatic. The stench in St Mark's prevented him from seeing all the treasures he had set out to see. But to return to the atrium – even in this century we recall that Thomas Mann's Aschen-bach lingered there while Tadzio deigned to turn his beautiful head, 'hunted him out, and looked at him'.* But in medieval times it was reserved for unbaptized persons and new converts to concentrate upon the Old Testament history depicted on ceiling and wall, before being admitted to the interior of the church.

The atrium mosaics have been described as one of the most immense and imposing commentaries that the Middle Ages made on the Old Testament. The subject is developed in an orderly transgression of sacred illusions, leading within the church to the anticipated coming of Christ and the sequel in the New Testament. The mosaics of the atrium are incidentally far easier to see than those in the body of the church. They have also fared better in spite of an earthquake of 1511 which reduced them to a very precarious condition. Certain it is from

Death in Venice.

stylistic evidence that the St Mark's iconography derived from Byzantine influences in the twelfth century. The following century witnessed the most intense period of the Venetian masters' mosaic school. A general increase in the size of the figures in relation to the background is noteworthy. The new pictorial manner begins with *The Ascension* in the central cupola of the transept. 'The Virtues and Beatitudes reveal a completely new plastic feeling, and the subjects are outside the Byzantine iconography scheme.'*

Whereas the Byzantine mosaics describe most vividly transcendental concepts and thoughts, capable of stirring us deeply, they are free from all emotion and totally abstracted from realism. In dispensing with natural images the pictures they form are reduced to scriptural formulae. Spiritual gestures are standardized. With the establishment of the Venetian craftsmen, a variety of expression and movement quite lacking in Byzantine mosaics becomes apparent. Even so, the Byzantine glance of the eyes and the stereotyped folds of the draperies are retained. Not till the arrival of the Renaissance mosaicists do we find a third dimension, perspective and play with spatial values.

The experts know how to identify mosaics assembled by the same craftsmen, even though these craftsmen were working to the designs of different artists. Recent restorations have revealed how early mosaicists, having drawn the outline of a design on a first layer of squared-off cement, applied a second layer of marble dust and pebblestone lime. The whole scene was then painted in colour and while the cement was soft the master and his men stuck in the appropriate *tesserae*. It is virtually impossible to see closely enough, even with binoculars, how the *tesserae* were chosen and applied to the ceilings and arches of St Mark's. No doubt it was the craftsmen's intention that this should be so. Therefore it is interesting to have some samples of old mosaics brought down to eye level in the museum. One feels that one is prying into the secrets of past artists.

*G. Musolini, *The Basilica of St Mark*.

Torcello Cathedral
and Santa Fosca

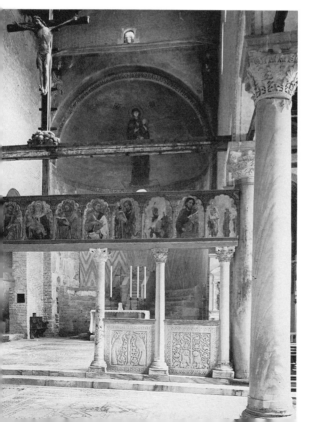

Torcello Cathedral:
choir and rood screen

St Mark's:
cupolas and pinnacles

St Mark's:
Pentecostal Dome in mosaic

The *tesserae* are mostly tiny, irregular, chipped fragments of jagged coloured stones. The painted ones have a gloss. The gold ones must have been dipped, not painted on the front, for the gold is nowhere spilt over the plaster interstices. Some were made of vitreous pulp painted or gilded on the back. Sometimes the *tesserae* were tilted in the cement in order to catch the anfractuosities of light from an obliquely facing window. A close-up view shows how impressionistic was the work. Fragments from a scene of *The Crucifixion*, which may well be the oldest mosaic of the interior, reveal that the technique employed resembles stippling, the *tesserae* being far from compact. Unfortunately it must be said that the mosaics for which St Mark's is justly famed can best be studied from coloured illustrations in books. When on the site you have to regard them, as you would vast tapestries, in semi-darkness – a glorious, mystical, hazy, decorative muddle. I cannot conceive how the primitive congregations in the Middle Ages, unable to read, had strong enough eyesight to follow the scriptural messages intended to be conveyed to their understanding.

Assuming that your eyesight is abnormally acute and that you have an authoritative and detailed guidebook in hand you should tackle the mosaics in the atrium from right to left. The atrium was built round three sides of the foot of the cross plan of St Mark's church, the right wing of which was in the sixteenth century closed and transformed into the Cappella Zen and the baptistery (on the south front). Like an arcade it is divided into bays by very wide arches, each bay with a domed roof and opening to the Piazza and Piazzetta dei Leoncini. Only the central bay on the Piazza front has no roof. It is the only part of the ninth-century building visible above ground. Its survival is due to the strange so-called *pozzo* (well), an open space fashioned to rise through the vault so as to receive daylight from the vast lunette window of the façade. Owing to this slipshod method of conveying light down to the entrance it was found necessary in subsequent ages to introduce several adventitious abutments to the structure. All the other atrium bays have hemispherical cupolas. The mosaics are by Venetian masters of the thirteenth century. They provide a unique cycle of Old

Testament stories from the Creation to the emigration of the Holy Family to Egypt.

Begin then with the Porta San Clemente (the right-hand entrance of the west façade) with its winged bronze doors, divided into twenty-eight rectangular panels of saints and inscriptions in silver. It came from Constantinople. The cupola and lunette mosaics of this atrium bay display *The Creation of the World* and the story of *Adam and Eve*. They date from 1200 – 1210 and were inspired by miniature illuminations of the sixth-century Cotton *Genesis* in the British Museum. Moving north-wards, you come to the next bay containing mosaics of *Noah and the Flood*. The central bay, with apse and bronze doors (Il Portale Maggiore) which echo the model of those of the Porta San Clemente and date from 1112–38, contains some of the oldest mosaics as well as *St Mark in Ecstasy* from a cartoon by Titian (1545). The adjoining divisive arch contains *The Tower of Babel* mosaics; the next *The Story of Abraham* (thirteenth century). Then comes the Porta Sant'Alippio, to which I have already referred. The next bay, already in the north wing, has *The Judgement of Solomon* and, on the cupola, *The Story of Joseph* (*circa* 1240); the last bay *The Story of Moses*, all thirteenth-century mosaics, but partly restored. And if you should leave the atrium by the Porta dei Fiori into the Piazzetta dei Leoncini it is imperative to look back at the Moorish arch with double inflected curve over the entrance. It belongs to the same wondrous century which witnessed the full flowering of the Venetian style derived from Byzantium, the Middle East, Ravenna, Genoa and Florence.

Of the atrium Old Testament mosaics my favourite scenes are those from *Noah's Life*. They are very entertaining. Noah's face is distinguishable throughout by the same rather over-hung jaw, whether he be drunk, sober or merely haranguing his sons. The storks, pelicans and strangely exotic creatures cajoled into the ark two by two, the raven pecking at offal in the blue waters, and Noah at the porthole letting loose the dove are enchanting. The *Tower of Babel* scenes are fascinating and instructive. A fourteenth-century workman climbs a ladder attached to scaffolding, a hod of bricks on his shoulder; another mixes lime for the mortar; three other men lift up a bucket of water. In *The Dream of Pharaoh's Butler and Baker*, the attitudes of the two servants, enveloped in a shroud denoting semi-consciousness, with eyes tight shut and bodies limp with sleep, are two-dimensional, astonishing, convincing and moving.

After imbibing the stories of the Old Testament in the atrium, the newly baptized, on entering the church, were meant to look behind them and contemplate the Great Arch of Paradise depicting *The Triumph of the Church over Eternity*, *The Exaltation of the Cross*, *The Salvation of the Elect* and *The Damnation of the Evil-doers*, taken from a cartoon by Tintoretto. Christ holds an open book with the inscription, 'I am the Gate of Life; let those who are mine enter by me'. Was this work the replacement of an early mosaic destroyed by earthquake, or merely by time's inexorable hand? The theme of the mosaics that follow is *The Exaltation of the Church of Christ*; and it is enacted in the progression of the three axial cupolas. The first, as it were at the foot of the cross, is the Pentecost cupola, illustrating *The Effusion of the Holy Spirit*. Through the prayers of the Apostles and the conversion of the people the Church is established. Rays of flame tie the Twelve to the Holy Dove in the eye of the circle. The central cupola over the conjunction of nave with transepts illustrates *The Ascension of the Living Christ*. The detail abounds in extraordinary little scenes. The Apostles, separated from one another by a tree, are so agitated that they seem to be dancing a ballet, their garments swishing, their hands stretched in affected attitudes, and their heads twisted in all directions, almost like marionettes. There is nothing static in the whole composition. The presbytery cupola illustrates *The Church's Fulfilment as Foretold by the Prophets*. In the eastern apse Christ is enthroned in blessing. The succession of Christian mysteries was deemed complete.

In the cupolas and on the arches and walls of the north and south transepts are to be found scenes of Our Lord and narratives relating to the New Testament – the Life of Our Lord and Mary, the Passion of Christ, and the lives of St Mark, St Peter and other saints specially venerated in Venice. In the right transept we have *The Discovery of St Mark's Body*. A section of the church is depicted with nave, columns and arches, gallery balustrade and domes. A sort of hinged door in a pillar miraculously opens so as to disclose the saint's coffin in an absurdly diminished scale, under the wondrous gaze of the doge. The praying congregation of standing nobles, plebeians and prostrate monks, their heads reverently inclined towards the altar, is touchingly demonstrative of medieval faith. In the right aisle *The Garden of Gethsemane* is very poignant: the Son's agonized communion with the Father, the look of resignation in his eyes, yet beseeching movement of his slender hands, while the Apostles are wrapped in slumber (the attitude of sleep was one in which the early mosaicists excelled); fritillaries and buttercups grow out of the rocky foreground as though to contrast the indifference of eternal nature to the traumas of the spirit. In the baptistery, Herod, in front of a Byzantine building, sits at a table spread with a white cloth. With his left hand he stretches for a flask of wine and with his right makes a gesture as though deprecating his implication in the Massacre of the Innocents and the beheading of St John the Baptist. Judging from the victuals before him, which include a dish with one innocent sprawled across it, some people will hardly wonder that he died of worms. Opposite the King's table the little figure of Salome, dressed in red and gold with white fur trimmings hanging from her elbows, dances while she holds the Baptist's head above her own. These pictures date from the fifteenth century.

The consequence of every square foot of wall space and vaulting space to boot being encrusted with mosaic, marble and precious stones, for the most part looted from the East, is that the interior of St Mark's lies in perpetual twilight, only disturbed by the flashes of Japanese cameras. When windows in the nave were blocked up to make room for more mosaics and it was thought fit to raise the cupolas on drums for better exterior effect, the original gallery floors over the aisles had to be removed in order to admit what little light was available to pavement level. Only the balustrades, supported by rows of small corbel heads, were allowed to remain. In lieu of the galleries a maze of cat-walks had to be added from time to time for the benefit of maintenance men.

On entering the church from the atrium by the great bronze doors bearing the dedication of Leo da Molino, who was Procurator in 1112, you must feel your way to a seat or plinth of a column, sit awhile and adjust those defective eyes to the darkness after the brightness of out-of-doors. Even when acclimatized the eyes, without the aid of a torch, do not allow note-taking. The curiously loud roar of unmuffled voices and the lack of incense detract from the devotional aura of one of the most sacred cathedrals in Europe. There is no longer evidence of much worship or reverence within St Mark's. No longer are groups at all hours of the day, as Ruskin noted, gathered before a shrine or altar in prayer. No one looks penitential. No one looks joyful. People merely look bewildered. They gape. No one appears to be examining detail as he might in an English cathedral, a fact which Ruskin found indicative of the average man's indifference to colour and disappointment with the small size of the interior. On this score he ought, Ruskin observed tartly, to keep away; for St Mark's is not to be judged by pure form. In St Mark's, he wrote, the architectural construction has become merged in the pictorial effect, 'and the whole edifice is to be regarded as a temple wherein to pray, then as itself a Book of Common Prayer, a vast illuminant missal, bound with alabaster instead of parchment, studied with porphyry pillars instead of jewels, and written within and without in letters of enamel and gold.'

But the average man today does not particularly relish being inside a prayer book. It takes time, a very long time, Ruskin assures us, before we can learn to appreciate the claims of the several parts of this church, the delicacy of their design, the perfection of their colour, the preciousness of their materials and their legendary interest. 'We must take some pains therefore, when we enter St. Mark's, to read all that is inscribed, or we shall not penetrate into the feeling either of the builder or of his times.' All very well, but how are we to read inscriptions if we cannot see them?

Gautier recognized our quandary and reconciled himself to it:

When the shadows thicken, and the sun thrusts no more than a ray of oblique light under the vaults and the cupolas, it produces strange impressions on the eyes ... Tawny lights reflect fleetingly from depths of gold. The little cubes of crystal squirm like wavelets of the sea under the setting sun. The contours of figures tremble in this flickering web; silhouettes, cut clean in half, suddenly seem to be in pain. The stiff folds of the dalmatics soften and dissolve and float; a mysterious life slips into these immobile byzantine personages. Staring eyes move, arms in a fixed Egyptian pose, loosen; halt feet begin to walk; the cherubim rustle into flight on their eight wings ...

Gautier's poetic reaction to the descending dusk is in fine contrast with the trite impressions of his contemporary, Charles Dickens, in the same circumstances. 'Unreal, fantastic, solemn, inconceivable throughout', he called the interior. Whereupon his radical mind turned with disapproval to the tortures which prisoners under the old doges had endured beneath the Ducal Palace.

I have always been surprised how much higher the interior seems than I would suppose from the outside. My impression is of being at the bottom of a submarine cave into which the flickering sun reflected from the mosaics is bravely trying to penetrate. For below a line formed by the springing of the slightly shouldered arches, walls and pillars, even the clusters of three columns on either side of the nave and the massive piers of the crossing are grey, like ruins submerged by water. The duplicated Greek cross suspended from the first nave dome, that of the Pentecost, immediately captures the attention with its twinkling oil holders and bulbous perforated bronze ball. It is the Lampadorio, a rich specimen of Byzantine jewellers' workmanship, but dimmed by age. The polychrome floor (eleventh century) on the right of the nave (the part on the left was levelled in the nineteenth century) is cracked and alarmingly undulating. It is like a magnificent old carpet woven in a multiplicity of faded colours. To right and left a pair of huge *aquasantieri* loom so high that you can barely reach to dip the finger. And now above the balustrades of the gallery with their incised panels (*plutei*) all is revealed to be gold, albeit dulled gold, from the gradual rise of the vault right up to the cupolas.

On your left, under the fourth arcade separating nave from aisle, is the polygonal Capitello del Crocifisso. It has a short pyramidal spire, very white, resting on round arches and columns of black and white African marbles with Byzantine capitals, partly gilded. The spirelet is surmounted by an enormous ovoid piece of agate. On the altar within the Capitello is a painted crucifix, much venerated, and possibly carried away from Constantinople in 1203. According to tradition it was once struck by an heretical pugilist. The agate, and not the pugilist, bled.

By now your eyes have accustomed themselves as well as they will ever do to the twilight. You may examine the columns of the nave as well as of the transepts. They reveal themselves, not as grey marble, but white alabaster veined with grey and amber. Each is of a single block, fifteen foot high. The capitals are remarkable for their sharp cutting. There is one with thistle- like leaves in open relief so that the light shines through it. Ruskin remarked upon the life in these capitals. To him they were more natural, and therefore more correct, than all the conventionalized Greek Corinthian capitals of the ancient world. He also admired the variety of their designs, even the separate sides of the same capital having a different pattern: 'No amount of illustration or eulogium would be enough to make the reader understand the perfect beauty of the thing itself, as the sun steals from interstice to interstice of its marble veil, and touches with the white lustre of its rays at midday the pointed leaves of its thirsty lilies.'

The crossing reached, the great rose window of the south transept filters the afternoon sun in bands of light which separate nave from presbytery. And from the crossing cupola, the Ascension, hangs a vase-shaped lantern. What looks like a pelican and must be a dove stands above a perforated ball. By a semi-circle of steps the iconastasis is reached. This masterpiece of Venetian Gothic was erected in 1394 to separate choir and chancel from the nave. The great screen is not, as it would be in a Greek Orthodox church, an impenetrable barrier. Over the *plutei* of its base and below the long rood which rests on eight columns, one can see into the presbytery. Polished, shining, polychrome, the frieze of semi-precious inlay twinkles as you walk past it. On either side of a dominant crucifix of bronze and silver stand, intensely solemn, the Twelve Apostles, and Mary and John the Baptist. Whereas each Apostle is made to hold the Holy Book, the Madonna's hands are free and the Baptist holds his head in one hand. These statues are the work of the Dalle Masegne brothers, Pierpaolo and Iacobello. Trained in the city, they remained active until 1410. Their sculpture was always carefully related to the architectural environment. Though severe in form it maintained contact with the natural world. Whereas sculpture in the northern Italian cities was, generally speaking, architectonic, a part of the structure, in Venice it had grown like barnacles upon a long submerged ship. The Contarini St Mark's at first had no sculpture; then with the oriental spoils sculpture accrued.

To left and right of the iconastasis are the two *amboni* or pulpits. That on the right, the '*Ambone* of the Reliquaries', is polygonal, an incredible structure of porphyry, polished and smooth like the surface of wine upon which one is tempted to breathe. Its vast weight is borne by stout columns with two lesser ones thrown underneath for extra support. From this *ambone* St Mark's sacred relics were exposed on holy days and here the newly elected doge showed himself to the people. The double *ambone* on the left is a stupendous feature of the church. From a fourteenth-century polygonal platform of rectangular panels rises a lectern of five semi-circles under a tester of bronze and marble, onion-shaped, ribbed and very oriental. From the eagle reading-desk the Gospel was read; from the lower platform the Epistle.

From the right of the porphyry *ambone* steps lead to the Cappella di San Clemente which used to be where the doge, slipping in from the Ducal Palace, would attend mass enthroned. This chapel is approached through its own little iconastasis of red Verona marble. On the architrave stand four statues, dated 1394, again by Gothic Venetian masters, the brothers Dalle Masegne. The brothers also contributed five statues to the iconastasis of the Cappella di San Pietro which balances that of San Clemente.

From the doge's passage you pass into the presbytery. You are beside the high altar under a *baldacchino* sustained by four extraordinary columns of oriental alabaster. They are crowded with diminutive carvings in this translucent material, ivory-coloured but white where fingered by generations of the devout and curious. The carvings, almost in the round, consist of nine stages of biblical and apochryphal figures under little shell-headed arcades, and date from about 1250. Under the high altar and behind a glass front is the sarcophagus of St Mark brought here from the crypt in 1835. All that you see is a large snow-white stone, or sarcophagus, with three indentations where once were iron cramps. Under glass, the sacred object resembles those spongy blocks of plastic packaging which forever float on the surface of the canals.

Behind the high altar is the famous Pala d'Oro, so highly illuminated by spot-lights that you have difficulty, jammed in a crowd of spectators within a narrow space, to find a stance where you are not blinded by the dazzling reflection. This astonishing screen of gold and jewellery, the rarest artefact of the Byzantine goldsmiths in existence, dates from the tenth to the fourteenth centuries. In other words it is composed of five stages, of which the first is said to have been commissioned by the saintly Doge Pietro Orseoli I in 976. Renewed and enriched by subsequent doges, each stage can be roughly dated by the architectural style of the miniature arcaded panels, some round-headed, some pointed, some ogival with tiny crockets and pinnacles, which frame religious scenes and figures – the deity, archangels, angels, apostles, prophets and Byzantine emperors and empresses – in enamel and laminated gold, encrusted with gems. Marvellous as is the workmanship, and exquisite the detail, the whole is too detailed, too intricate and too rich for my taste. It is perhaps not surprising that the Pala d'Oro was spared from plunder by Napoleon's minions who did not believe so pretentious a work could be genuine. Had these ignorant persons known the truth, the Pala d'Oro would have been removed to Paris or melted down. More to my taste are the bronze statuettes of the bearded evangelists by Iacopo Sansovino, seated on the balustrade to the right of the altar and dated 1514. They and the door, also by Sansovino, leading from the north side of the presbytery apse to the sacristy, are unexcelled by any other comparable art of the Italian high Renaissance.

Sansovino, one of the greatest Italian sculptors and architects, was not Venetian by birth. After the sack of Rome in 1528 he fled to Venice where he remained until his death in 1570. I repeat that the Venetians had the sense to make him Proto, or architect, to St Mark's. Sansovino positively prevented the church from tumbling to ruin. He was a prodigious worker. He built the Marcian Library opposite the Doges' Palace and designed the Procuratie Nuove on the south side of the Piazza. With infinite care he adapted each of his buildings to its site and purpose. His contemporary Vasari has left a description of his person and deportment. As a young man he was so handsome, well dressed and well groomed that he was beloved by ladies of all ranks and sorts. In old age his appearance was venerable. He kept his fine figure and upright carriage till the end. This was no wonder for he lived abstemiously and would often confine his meals to three cucumbers and half a lemon.

Sansovino's bronze sacristy door on the curve of the apse was his last masterpiece. On the two wings are bas-relief panels of Christ deposited in the tomb and the Resurrection. In the latter panel the upward movement to the left, made by St Joseph of Aramathea dragging Christ's limp body from the grave, and the serried row of veiled mourning women, induce feelings of extreme pathos and hope. Also included on the door are little portrait heads in the round, of the evangelists and prophets in the likeness of Aretino, Titian, Veronese, Palladio, and the sculptor himself.

Until the first quarter of the eighteenth century nearly 200 lagoon towers could be counted from Malamocco to Torcello. AD 912 is given as the year in which St Mark's campanile foundations were dug. In 939 the shaft was begun. Seventy-six years later the belfry was reached. What happened between then and the late twelfth century when the tower was completed is uncertain. In 1329 the four-sided pyramidal pinnacle was twice destroyed by lightning, and twice repaired. From the fourteenth to the sixteenth century the torture of the *chega* was a common sight for the citizens of Venice. Malefactors were suspended for days on end from the top of the tower in a wicker cage, fed occasionally with bread and water let down to them on a rope, and jeered and insulted by the passers-by. A more welcome spectacle – although God knows whether human beings do not secretly prefer to witness acts of cruelty – was the *volo d'angelo*, or *del Turco*, held on the last Thursday of the Carnival. On a rope stretched from the belfry to the *bucintoro* or ducal barge moored in St Mark's basin, an acrobat would descend, and on reaching the doge present him with a bunch of flowers.

On 26 March 1511 a severe earthquake caused the big bells in the belfry to ring themselves for the space of a miserere and a little longer, thus adding further terror to the stricken citizens of Venice. In 1514 a new belfry of solid Renaissance shape, and no longer of wood, was built by the distinguished mason, Pietro Buon. To the sound of pipes and drums the gilt angel was hoisted on the topmost pinnacle. Celebrations were accompanied by much drinking of milk and more of wine. Several thunderbolts however caused repeated damage to this prominent landmark. In 1653 a disastrous thunderbolt caused the whole belfry to be restored by the architect Baldassare Longhena.

Already Sansovino's jewel-like Loggetta was nestling at the east foot of the great square tower. There is something a trifle incongruous in so delicate a temple – for that is what it amounts to – clinging to the bottom of a cliff. When Sansovino finished it in 1540 it was, taken on its own merits, a beautiful building, albeit slightly over-adorned with sculpture; and lighter without the balustrade imposed upon it in the seventeenth century. It was fated to be crushed to atoms in 1902. At 10 o'clock in the morning of 14 July of that year, the campanile, the oldest and most striking architectural feature of Venice, cracked from top to bottom, split asunder as though to disclose St Mark's body, and subsided in a heap of bricks, dust and debris. The accident did not happen with such suddenness that a passer-by was unable to take a photograph of the process. The corner of Sansovino's Marcian Library was badly damaged and his Loggetta was to all intents and purposes destroyed. A captain of a merchant ship out at sea, after witnessing the collapse through his binoculars, was either so shocked or convinced that he had lost his senses, for the sea was utterly calm and the sky serene, that he threw himself from the bridge and did away with himself.

The following year the rebuilding of the campanile began, and by 1912 it was finished to everyone's and posterity's satisfaction. The Loggetta too, shattered piece by piece, was meticulously re-assembled, but somehow still retains the appearance of a fake. Except for the great Marangona, which escaped unhurt, all the old bells had to be re-cast.

SANTA MARIA GLORIOSA
DEI FRARI

1340–1443

If one is walking north from, say, the Accademia, having crossed a series of *rii*, or narrow canals, one is apt to pause on the steep bridge over the rather less narrow Rio di Ca' Foscari (that ominous name in Venetian medieval history). There, straight ahead, rises over the roof-tops a great, square, brick tower, seen diagonally, with a slight lean to the right. It is the campanile of the Frari church. It is very impressive against the blue sky, with its vertical recessed panels of blind and cusped heads forming what the Touring Club Italiano guidebook delights in describing as *lesene*. Strictly speaking the word *lesena* means a pilaster, which is a shallow pier or half column projecting from the wall of a classical building. Here in this fourteenth-century campanile what look like projecting strips are in reality parts of the basic wall. It is the panels in between which are recessed. The deeply burnt brick stages are divided by thin horizontal bands, or string courses, of white Istrian stone. Over a belfry of three open arcades and protected by a stone balustrade is a delicious cupola of octagonal shape under a frieze of terracotta heads, like one of those red paper frills which decorate a bought wedding cake, the whole crowned by an ogee roof and lead finial. This roof of the second highest tower in Venice was formerly gilded in order to catch the rising and setting sun as a beacon to ships at sea. At midday and at sunset a deep booming bell tolls from the belfry; whereupon the church doors are unceremoniously shut behind the last loitering visitor to the church.

From the Foscari Bridge the Frari appears deceptively near. But the moment one has descended to the other side of the wide *rio* the campanile is lost to view. Fairly soon however one emerges into the south corner of the Campo San Rocco. Immediately above one soars the campanile, which is contiguous to the great basilica.

There are two stances whence one may obtain the best views of the Frari church at close range. The first, if one turns sharply left, is from the steps of the Scuola di San Rocco, that amazing repository of Tintoretto canvases. What one obliquely sees is two stages of the central hexagonal apse, perforated by thin, lancet-like windows with pointed heads. Ruskin found these apse windows precursors of those of the first-floor arcades of the Ducal Palace, with this difference: whereas the windows of the former building have quatrefoils over the heads of the arches, which are sustained by thin shafts, the arcades of the latter have quatrefoils directly over the shafts, which are accordingly more solid. From this he deduced that the Ducal Palace arcades were a development of the Frari apse windows as a result of architectural experiment. The main reason for the alteration was that the weight above was thus thrown between the quatrefoils, and not on them. Again, whereas in the Frari the lintels are formed of a separate block of horizontal stone, in the Ducal Palace the lintels are made of the same piece of stone as the quatrefoils, only with a joint cut through the lintel and centre of each quatrefoil.

The second stance is reached by turning right from the Campo di San Rocco and following the bulk of the church into the open Campo dei Frari. With one's back to the *rio* of that name, one confronts the so-called west façade (actually it faces north-east) and north (actually south-east) elevation, against which raucous youths will undoubtedly be kicking a football while their girlfriends busily deface the domed well-head with *graffiti*, from little syringes of coloured paints.

While there are more spectacular Gothic 'west' façades in northern Europe, those of Venice have a simplicity and gauntness which are appealing. *Lesene* again, and these four really are pilasters of a sort, for they project from the main surface and run from ground level to skyline. The inner pair and the central apex of the façade carry slender aedicules, typical Venetian Gothic, with spire-like canopies supported by delicate shafts. Silhouetted against the sky, for once they do not shelter figures and can be enjoyed unencumbered. The façade apex, a convoluted gable over the nave which tumbles down the aisles, presents an outline almost Baroque, not diminished by the shadow of a pediment above the enormous circular window. One can even extend the term Baroque to Rococo in describing the delicate frieze of corbels, each with a tiny pendant of Istrian stone, which surrounds the entire body of the church. The vertical accent is again emphasized by the pointed arch of the central doorway, flanked by figures on slender pedestals, of the *Madonna with Child* in her arms, and *St Francis of Assisi* in the manner of Bartolomeo Buon (mid-fifteenth century); and, crowning the arch, *The Risen Christ* by Alessandro Vittoria (late sixteenth century).

The austerity of the composition is quite in accord with the precepts of the Order of the Friars Minor for whom the monastic church was built between 1340 and 1443. That Order, founded by St Francis in 1209, was distinguished by insistence upon complete poverty. Thirteen years later the Friars were established in Venice where Doge Iacopo Tiepolo gave them a tract of land on which to build. Their first modest church was replaced by the present one, not because the Brothers had relaxed their vows and become vainglorious, but because their congregations were ever-increasing. The site was propitious for so huge an edifice because, unlike the south-eastern quarter of the Dorsoduro, the clay belt under the Frari is, according to Horatio Brown, from twenty to twenty-five feet thick. The clay in its turn rests on a bed of shifting sand whose depth has not been probed.

Entry to the monastic church is by the door on the (ecclesiastical) north side, and literally through the colossal Pesaro monument, which we shall return to on our way out. The interior is undeniably impressive, or as the great Victorian architect George Street puts it, 'The internal effect of the church is much finer than its west front would lead one to expect'. He reminds us that the architect – an anonymous Brother of the Order – was working in a country where light was something to be kept at bay, so he was unable to revel in the glowing colours which the architects of northern lands so desperately sought after. This is only partially true. On the other hand he lived in a country where artists abounded. He probably took it for granted that his bare walls would with time be filled with colourful mosaics, frescoes or paintings of scriptural stories. In the meantime the fourteenth-century architect intended the beauty of his church to rely upon its correct proportions and the simplicity of the quadripartite groining of the vault. He certainly did not foresee that his creation was to become, like Westminster Abbey, crammed with monuments of the illustrious laity, some reaching right up to the springing of the arches.

Indeed on entry the space seems limitless. Nave and aisles are upheld by eight enormous round columns. The sharply pointed vaults are echoed by the pointed arches separating nave from aisles. The criss-cross supporting beams from capital to capital of the columns do not somehow detract from the verticality of the structure. Their timber sides and soffits are painted in arabesques on a mustard brown. The pavement, composed of red, green and grey marble squares laid diamond-wise may not be medieval. It certainly lends colour. The once spartan walls are a veritable shrine of Gothic to Neo-classical memorials by great artists: Donatello, Buon, Sansovino, Vittoria, Barthel, Canova, among sculptors; and Giovanni Bellini, Titian, the two Vivarini, and Palma il Giovane among painters.

The Frari shares with the church of SS Giovanni e Paolo (familiarly called San Zanipolo) the distinction of being the Venetian empire's two mausoleums of her heroes. It is hard to say which is the more important or more likeable. Robert Browning after years of residence in Venice could never make up his mind. He only knew that he preferred the monuments to the paintings which either contained. After a good deal of reflection, my choice in spite of the incomparable setting of San Zanipolo beside the early Renaissance Scuola di San Marco and the Colleoni statue in the foreground, is the Frari. The latter contains under one roof the greatest assortment of

The Frari: nave and choir

La Madonna dell' Orto

San Nicolò dei Mendicoli: interior

Ca' d'Oro

architectural, sculptural and pictorial creations of genius in the choir screen, the statuary that adorns it, and the Titian *Assumption* which looms behind and above it – to form a unit of unsurpassable pre-eminence in terms of world art.

Immediately on your left on entry the stupendous vision breaks upon you. The Friars' choir is contained by four piers composed of clustered columns extending from the nave without breaking the height of the vaulting. On three sides it is separated from the main body of the church by the incomparable marble screen, still preserved in its original position since construction by the Buon and finished by the Lombardi family in 1475. Thus it is transitional Gothic in form and Renaissance in execution. In two stages between pilasters, eight panels are filled with reliefs of patriarchs and Old Testament prophets and the four doctors of the church. The encompassing foliage is pricked out in gold. Entrance is through a raised classic arch carrying a bronze crucifix flanked by statues of the *Madonna* and *St John the Evangelist*, works of Pietro Lombardo. Over the rich entablature stand *The Apostles with St Anthony and St Francis*. At the angles are projecting pulpits apparently added in the eighteenth century and considered awkward by some, though not by me.

Within are the most beautiful choir stalls in the world, 124 in number. Under Gothic cresting a shell hood pricked with gold shelters each stall. Within each stall is carved in relief a panel of a different saint; and below each saint an intarsia panel, depicting landscapes and architectural perspectives, no one view resembling another. Finally, at floor level a row of misericords, their backs worked in intarsia. A lifetime could be spent in examining the detailed variety of this composition which transcends craftsmanship and raises intarsia to an art vying with architecture, sculpture, painting and music. The creator of this magnificent composition was Marco Cozzi, who left his signature on it in 1468.

As I have already indicated, behind the choir and visible through the arch from the nave hangs Titian's immense canvas of *The Assumption*. This masterpiece was expressly commissioned by the prior of the monastery in 1516 for the central apse over the high altar. It was completed two years later notwithstanding the artist experiencing much interference and occasional disapproval from the Brothers. Never can a better justification be found for leaving a great picture on the site for which it was intended than here. It is true that before electricity enabled it to be adequately illuminated the painting must have been hard to see by day (as well as night), placed against the dazzling light from the long windows of the apse. Charles de Brosses, while praising it in 1740, complained that as well as being '*mal soigné, fort noirçi*', it was '*placé dans un mauvais jour où l'on le voit mal*'.

The composition, within the gold frame and architectural reredos designed for it, is divided into three distinct horizontal planes. In the lowest the Apostles in various attitudes of amazement and bewilderment are dominated by the figure, seen from behind, of St Andrew, wearing a scarlet robe under a shock of hair, his arms upraised as though speeding the vision on its way. In the middle plane the Madonna, likewise clad in scarlet and a deep blue coat, is being lifted into the sky by a crescent of winged cherubs on a cloud. 'She soars heavenward,' in the words of Bernard Berenson, 'not helpless in the arms of angels, but borne up by the fulness of life within her, and by the feeling that the universe is naturally her own, and that nothing can check her course . . . [The angels] are embodied joys, acting on our nerves like the rapturous outbursts of the orchestra at the end of *Parsifal*.'

Indeed Titian's *Assumption* so moved Wagner when he saw it that 'my old powers revived as though by a sudden flash of inspiration', which induced him at once to compose *Die Meistersinger*. His old powers had incidentally been rendered dormant by pique. For when dining in the Piazza during the Austrian occupation and listening to his overtures being played by the municipal orchestra, not a single Italian in the audience applauded.

In the third and highest plane we have God the Father brooding over the scene. From a distance he looks like a great bat with outstretched wings: in actuality the everlasting arms. The expression of the tilted face framed in brown hair and greyish beard streaming in the celestial wind is in fact one of profound benignity and compassion. The deep tonality and vibrant colouring of the immense picture has the effect of a warming furnace in some vast medieval hall.

Let us now move to the west door of the Frari church which is the conventional starting point of every guidebook, observing before we proceed from right to left the Baroque monument over the door to *Giralomo Garzoni*, who was killed in the siege of Negroponte in 1688. His stiff effigy in sumptuous white and black marble wears a wig which looks as though it were made of rock. Below him and on the south side of the door Tullio Lombardo's monument (1524) to Senator *Pietro Bernardo* is a slightly top-heavy conception in three parts. Ruskin was not entirely wrong in declaring: 'nothing can be more detestable or mindless in general design, or more beautiful in execution', if we modify the adjective 'detestable'. The Senator's sons added the top part as an afterthought. Note however the fine bas-relief, the head of the Medusa and the eagle with wings outspread.

The first aisle chapel displays a large canvas by Francesco Rosa of *St Anthony of Padua* reviving a dead man in testimony of the father's innocence. The brawny, sunburnt figures are in powerful contrast with the pallid flesh of the resurrected man in the foreground. Standing in a holy water stoup of elegant design a bronze figure of *Mansuetude* (Meekness) (1593) holds a tiny lamb with her right hand. It is by Gerolamo Campagna, one of the last Renaissance sculptors before the Baroque age set in. He was a Veronese whose figures, all of high quality, are to be found in several Venetian churches.

We soon come to the monument to Titian, a triumphal arch dating from 1852, an academic Canovaesque hang-over but not contemptible. It is the only known case of an artist's monument displaying in relief representations of his pictures, the central one here being *The Assumption*. The monument to *Amerigo d'Este*, a captain in the war of Candia (1660) is another example of commonplace figure sculpture which gives the Baroque a bad name. It must be admitted that many such post-Bernini effigies are stiff, pompous and incredibly puffed up. The statue of

St Jerome is a very different affair. Alessandro Vittoria, a contemporary of Campagna, came from Trento, was a pupil of Sansovino and is one of the great portrait sculptors which Palladio's generation produced. Inspired by Michelangelo's *Moses*, *St Jerome* is extremely forceful. Instead of the usual old spindle-shanks, Vittoria's model, said to be Titian himself, is vigorous and muscular with large strong hands. The sweep of the saint's beard and falling garment anticipates the Baroque. The ubiquitous lion is made to laugh as though enjoying the joke which is humanity. Palma il Giovane's *St Catherine of Alexandria* is a swirling confusion of arms, legs and broken wheels. The monument to the *Bishop of Pola* by Antonio Pittone (1708) is an early eighteenth-century improvement on the worn-out funerary Baroque of the late *seicento*. A lively relief portrait within a frame held by an angel in flight supports, with the help of a *putto*, a scroll of the bishop's virtues. A sepulchral urn tomb by Giovanni Maria Mosca, a concert of horizontal lines, is in the most sparing style of early Renaissance sculpture.

Opposite this monument and against the wall of the choir a low walnut chest with dreary panels is remarkable for its length. Turning right into the transept you are struck by a vast monument on the west wall to *Iacopo Marcello*, a casualty in the assault against Gallipoli. It is by Pietro Lombardo and his school. The doorway to the sacristy is framed by a triumphal arch monument to *Benedetto Pesaro*, a captain killed at Corfu in 1503. To the left the monument by Iacopo della Quercia, famous sculptor from distant Siena, to *Paolo Savelli* (1405), a Roman patrician, in gilt and polychrome wood, is the first equestrian statue of a *condottiere* in Venice, antedating Verocchio's famous Colleoni. Poor Thomas Coryate complained that the epitaph was 'in such obsolete and difficult characters' that he could not read it. No wonder. And finally on the right of the sacristy entrance the gilded wall-sarcophagus (*urna pensile* the guidebook calls it) of the *Beato Pacifico*, St Francis's legendary companion, is an example of the common use of sculptured terracotta when good stone for carving had to be brought from afar. The date 1437 of the Pacifico's burial is discernible underneath the sarcophagus.

In the sacristy which resembles a little church and was built by the Pesaro family in the middle of the fifteenth century stands the tabernacle of the *Reliquary of the Blood of Christ*, an extremely handsome Baroque shrine (1711) in coloured marbles. Under a central umbrella tester the holy relic, brought to Venice from Constantinople in 1479, is preserved within a panel of rare marbles framed like a gilt carved drawing-room mirror. On every Palm Sunday it is carried in procession. Flanking it are marble relief panels of *The Deposition* and *Entombment* by Francesco Penso, called Cabianca (1665–1737). The pair of gold angels above the tester suspending lanterns on long chains are by Andrea Brustolon, the famous *ébéniste*, a suite of whose carved furniture you will be seeing in the Ca' Rezzonico.

Still in place on the altar for which it was painted and so part and parcel of the whole is Giovanni Bellini's triptych in its original elaborate frame. Winged mermaids support candelabra with their hands and tails. Madonna and Child painted within a feigned niche appear to be in the round. The face of the serene Madonna is that of an ordinary country girl in the joy of motherhood; that of the Child a precocious pudding. Superb is the figure of St Mark, a crozier in his right hand; in his left his Gospel thrust towards the spectator with a gesture implying, 'Read and digest, or be damned.' At the Madonna's feet one angel plays a lute; another, a laurel wreath round his forehead, a flute. Of this triptych Taine remarked, '*Toutes ces figures ont vécu . . . On ne pouvait s'empêcher de croire en eux*'; Henry James was even more laudatory:

> Nothing in Venice is more perfect than this. It is impossible to imagine anything more finished or more ripe. It is one of those things that sum up the genius of a painter, the experience of a life, the teaching of a school. It seems painted with molten gems, which have only been clarified by time, and it is as solemn as it is gorgeous, and as simple as it is deep.

Prominent in the adjoining Sala Capitolare is the fourteenth-century monument to *Francesco Dandolo*, Venice's fiftieth doge, whose persistence had induced the pope to withdraw excommunication of the city by hiding under His Holiness's dinner-table in Avignon, embracing his knees and refusing to let go until he got what he wanted. Through the sacristy window you can get a view of the cloister of the Holy Trinity, designed by Andrea Palladio and carried out after his death. The Doric arcade of white Istrian stone has a balustraded upper walk. In the garth a well is sheltered by an early eighteenth-century arch with an explosion of sculpture by Francesco Cabianca on the crest.

Returning to the church you come to the first of the eight apses of the east end, namely the Cappella Bernardo. Within a rich Renaissance frame is a polyptych signed by Bartolomeo Vivarini (1482). The Virgin enthroned with the Child on her knee is flanked by St Andrew accompanied by St Nicholas of Bari, and St Paul by St Peter; in the upper part lies a half-length figure of the Dead Christ. Lorenzetti judges the work to be 'strongly stylized with vigorous use of colour'.

The third apsidal chapel contains within an altar-piece a wooden figure of *St John the Baptist* by Donatello. It is one of the most moving pieces of carving in Christendom. Gilded and painted, the Baptist is represented wild-eyed and emaciated, yet intensely vigorous. Hair straggles below his shoulders. He wears a skirt of shaggy hide and a tattered yellow cloak. His mouth is in the act of announcing the Coming. *'Ecce Agnus Dei'* is inscribed on the scroll held loosely in his left hand; with his right he emphasizes the terrible message and demand for instant repentance and baptism from his unseen audience. One almost quails lest he will catch one's own eye and advance from his tabernacle to seize one by the hair. Donatello's original paint was uncovered in a restoration of 1973; also the master's signature and the date 1438.

In the central apse of the high altar, on either side of Titian's *Assumption*, are two Renaissance tombs, facing one another. On the right is that of *Francesco Foscari*, one of Venice's greatest and most tragic doges, immortalized by musicians and dramatists, including Lord Byron. Having extended the boundaries of the Republic he was deposed by the Council of Ten for treachery on 23 October 1457 and died on the 30th to the sound of bells announcing the election of his successor. The monument marks a point of departure in Venetian funerary sculpture in that the figures are life-like as opposed to symbolical. The tomb chest base is heavy Gothic. The beautiful tent canopy with falling drapery and traces of gold in the lining held open by two warriors so as to reveal the doge's recumbent effigy might be mistaken for a Rococo conception but was actually first introduced by Donatello on his tomb of Baldassare Coscia in the baptistery in Florence. At Doge Foscari's head and feet stand four Cardinal Virtues with their attributes. It is impossible to believe that these most moving, and indeed visibly moved figures, whose very clothes, gestures and attitudes are natural and free, were not portraits of individuals, even members of his family who mourned the old doge's death. The sculptor of this work of art has long been called Antonio Bregno, one of Bartolomeo Buon's younger collaborators. A recent scholar, Miss A. M. Schulz, convincingly attributes it to Nicolò di Giovanni Fiorentino, a pupil of Donatello, between 1457 and 1467.

On the facing wall is the enormous tomb of *Nicolò Tron*. The galaxy of conventionalized figures occupying four stages under a semi-circular arch is not at first glance pleasing. On the bottom stage the great, coarse merchant doge stands, the first of his rank to be represented in an upright position on a tomb. After a while one is impressed by the simple verticality of the design which the vast size renders almost aspirant. Moreover the surrounding drapery and armorial shields painted on the bare wall somehow soften the starkness of this massive block of masonry. The Tron tomb is the work of Antonio Rizzo of Verona, who settled in Venice in 1466. He is more renowned for his architecture than his sculpture. The alternations of advance and recess of the Tron monument are certainly architectural.

The next apsidal chapel of St Francis contains the altar-piece by Bernardino Licinio of the *Madonna and Child* enthroned above a cluster of saints, of whom St Francis genuflecting and mysteriously supporting a lily without holding it, is the most prominent. In the seventh apsidal Chapel of the Milanese Brotherhood, within a rich altar-piece of 1503, *St Ambrose*

Enthroned was begun by the painter Alvise Vivarini and finished by Marco Basaiti. The Milanesian or Ambrosian rite, while generally following the Roman canon of the mass, differs in several niggling particulars.

Lastly, and eighth in number, is the Cappella Corner, a later addition to the apsidal complex. It also contains masterpieces but is so dark that unless the sacristan can be persuaded to turn on the lights, little can be observed. Facing the entrance is the monument to *Federico Corner* (d.1378), greatly esteemed by the Republic for saving his country during the war between Chioggia and Genoa. It is by a follower of Donatello. A handsome angel holds in front of him a large scroll of the deceased's virtues against background frescoes of *putti*, attributed to Mantegna. On the font is a statue of *St John the Baptist*, seated, in a swooning attitude. The beautiful head is of a gentle, almost gentlemanly youth, in absolute contrast to Donatello's wild man of the wilderness whom we have recently noticed.

The most treasured work of art here, however, is the triptych of *St Mark*, to whom the Corner chapel was dedicated by its donors. This altar-piece bears the signature of Bartolomeo Vivarini, the uncle of Alvise, and the date 1474. The gilded wooden frame is flamboyantly Gothic whereas the throne on which the saint is seated is of early Renaissance design. Here we have one of many instances of paintings depicting architecture in a style seemingly in advance of the date of the picture's composition. The broad-browed bruiser Evangelist is in ludicrous contrast with the effeminate angels scratching away at stringed instruments at his feet and squatting demurely, with folded arms, at his side.

Returning to the north door by way of the aisle you see the second Titian masterpiece loom into view. *The Madonna di Ca' Pesaro* is framed within a marble altar of the Lombardo family's manufacture. This canvas was painted between 1519 and 1526 to the order of Iacopo Pesaro, Bishop of Paphos (seen kneeling to the left of the picture), after defeating the Turks in battle. Other members of the family kneel on the opposite side. Berenson observed that the donor and his family were not overcome with that awe and devotion which might be expected in the circumstances, but looked worldly and too pleased with themselves. Certainly the little boy is not even attending to the vision but turning round to gaze at the painter. In this composition Madonna and Child for the first time do not occupy a central position. Yet such was the skill of the artist that in his grouping of the participants he draws the eye to the unassuming Mother (for whom the model was Titian's wife Celia, soon to die in childbirth) and Child, not enthroned, but sitting on the base of one of two massive columns.

Even these monoliths and the central figure of St Peter do not, vulgarly speaking, steal the limelight. St Peter with open book, undeniably the most prominent figure, is magnificent in a deep blue robe and yellow drapery. Below him a single key is painted in perspective upright against a step. Whereas the Pesaro family are static, if inattentive, the divine and saintly participants are full of movement. The crimson armorial banner of Pope Alexander VI and the Turkish prisoner's white turban, like a swirl of whipped cream, the brilliant and plangent colours of the garments, the apricot dress of the Madonna, the russet brown habit of St Francis put this picture at the apex of Venetian painting.

The Pesaro family may have been a vainglorious lot. The monument to *Doge Giovanni* (he reigned but two years), erected in 1669, through which we entered the church by the north door, is almost overpowering in its swagger. The design is attributed to Longhena, the execution of the sculpture to the German Melchior Barthel, and the bronze skeletons clutching scrolls to Bernardo Falcone from Lugano. It is a wonderful example of Baroque glorification of the individual, especially if he be patrician, rather than the Deity or even the state. The black heads and arms of four Moors standing on plinths are crushed by the weight of an entablature bearing an upper stage in which the doge sits enthroned under a red marble baldaquin, surrounded by allegorical female figures in white marble. It is a relief to one's sense of vicarious pain that the Moors are at least given thick cushions, albeit made of Carrara, for their heads. Over the upper cornice the muzzles of two heavy cannons add to the weight of the stupendous structure. J. G. Links in *Venice for Pleasure* finds this monument terrifying.

A greater contrast of style could hardly be found between the Baroque Pesaro tomb and the Neo-classical mausoleum to *Canova* a few bays away. Raised from the pavement on three steps and protected by a slender railing, the pyramid is simplicity itself. The model was originally made by Canova in 1794 for Titian's tomb; but funds could not be raised to carry it out. When Canova lay dying in October 1822 the Accademia d'Arte, wishing to enshrine the great sculptor's heart in a worthy monument, adopted his model for the abandoned Titian tomb. Venice and Europe subscribed generously. Five of Canova's pupils carried out the work. When it was completed in 1827 the porphyry urn containing Canova's heart was placed inside the mausoleum. Through the central door left ajar the veiled figure of Sculpture holding a canister of oil is about to enter, followed by Painting and Architecture with bowed heads. Little *putti* guide them with lit torches. On the other side of the door the genius of Canova in the form of a sexless youth reclines with extinguished torch and the winged lion of Venice stretches docile limbs on the cold white marble steps. Above the door two angels in relief carry a portrait of Canova circumscribed by a snake, the symbol of immortality.

It is not surprising that people of taste in mid- and late-Victorian times regarded Canova's mausoleum with distaste and even contempt. To them it was pagan and entirely lacking in Christian symbolism. 'Consummate in science, intolerable in affection, ridiculous in conception, null and void to the uttermost in invention and feeling', were Ruskin's sentiments. W. D. Howells, the American Consul in Venice, was too indifferent even to comment on its demerits. He was more interested in watching the Friars' black cat, which lived in the sacristy, emerge at nightfall, make straight for Canova's tomb and pass through the door, foraging for mice and rats.

LA MADONNA DELL'ORTO

1392–1483

The Madonna dell'Orto stands on the most northerly and most remote (that is to say from St Mark's Piazza) of the islets that form Venice. It comes within the ward (or *sestiere*) of Cannaregio. One may say that only the two bridges over the wide Rio della Madonna (there is none over the Rio degli Zecchini to the west) keep it from floating away into the Lagoon, to which it is exposed on the north and east. In the latter quarter the islet is occupied by the slightly sinister and certainly haunted Casino degli Spiriti and its large melancholy garden.

Very much smaller than the Frari, and without a transept, the Madonna dell'Orto was originally built in 1348 in basilican form to the designs of a Franciscan monk called Fra Tiberio from Parma, and dedicated to St Christopher whose knee-cap is preserved on one of the altars. Less than thirty years later a tiresome thing happened. A statue of the *Madonna and Child* made a miraculous descent in a neighbouring orchard (*orto*). It was at once carried in triumph to the church where it was duly venerated. Its fame became so widespread and its visitors so numerous that in the last decade of the fourteenth century St Christopher's had not only to be renamed, but rebuilt.

The very statue is preserved today in the Cappella di San Mauro, approached from the right aisle of the church. And a sorry affair it is too. Colossal in size – it must have descended heavily to account for its dreadfully damaged condition – it is of rough stone that looks like plaster. The snood that covers the head and much besides has been repaired. The countenance of the Madonna, though lumpish, is benign and a drip is carved on the end of her nose. Like many another Venetian church the

Madonna dell'Orto has undergone its bad times. In 1855 it was handed over to the army and used in succession as stables, a depot for straw, and a powder magazine. It was reopened for public worship fourteen years later. It was badly restored in 1874 and not so badly restored in 1932. It was again restored, this time well, by the British Flood Relief Fund in 1969.

The Madonna dell'Orto is an interesting example of a late fourteenth-century church begun just before the Renaissance. The rosy brick façade of the nave bears resemblances to that of the Frari in the ogival-headed doorway, incorporating a tympanum of porphyry, large round window, lavish terracotta frieze and three aedicules (shrines) of white Istrian stone. The two aedicules over the aisle façades have not prevented the figures they shelter from getting black. Sir John Pope-Hennessy states that both the father and son masons Buon were engaged on the façade as early as 1392. Work must in this case have proceeded slowly, for not only were the Gothic transomed windows of the aisle wings added in the mid-fifteenth century but the free-standing portal was commissioned from Bartolomeo Buon in 1460, to be executed in 1483. On the other hand the *Twelve Apostles* within the sloping niches of the aisles are the work of the Dalle Masegne brothers in the 1390s. The statue of *St Christopher* crowning the entrance arch is however mid-fifteenth century. Christopher plods through a stream bent beneath the weight of the Child Christ who clutches a tuft of the saint's hair. The statue is attributed by A. M. Schulz to Nicolò di Giovanni Fiorentino. *The Virgin* and *Archangel Gabriel* over the columns may be the works of the young Antonio Rizzo.

Altogether the façade is one of the most highly decorated and interesting in Venice; and the view of it dominating the miniature *campo* is enchanting. Part of the left aisle is in typical Venetian manner, because sites are scarce, obscured by the little Scuola dei Mercanti, actually projected by Palladio in 1570. Over this odd conjunction rises the campanile, one of the best preserved of the *quattrocento*. Above the three belfry openings a tympanum is pierced by an eye window. Above the tympanum the curious bulbous dome contributes that oriental touch which illustrates Venice as the artistic meeting place of

East with West. Admittance to the beautiful monastic cloisters, with slightly pointed openings to a deserted garth, is not readily granted. It is a pity because they afford the best view of the body of the church. But since the cloisters are now used for storing timber the attitude of the custodians is understandable, if regrettable.

Augustus Hare recommends that this church should be visited after 2 p.m. when the afternoon sun, reflected from the lagoon waters, inundates the interior, which is, he concedes, very handsome. It is also rendered bright and cheerful by the polygonal apse of the presbytery. One is struck by the slender grey and green Greek columns of the nave which to Hugh Honour's eye resemble 'grey watered silk'. Indeed they seem to ripple as one advances, like the gentle surge of the shallow lagoon waters, against the pink brick walls of the aisles. The Gothic capitals of volutes and rosettes roughly carved carry pointed arches and also support those ubiquitous wooden cross-beams. Whether or not a groined vault was intended for the nave, the actual ship's keel roof is a later and effective ceiling.

Immediately to the right on entry, a marble group (school of Antonio Rizzo) of *Madonna and Child* is touching in its simplicity. Love is written on the features of the Virgin's face and gentleness in the long slender fingers. In the first chapel Cima da Conegliano's superb painting of *St John the Baptist and Saints* is one of the best known works by that master. The Baptist standing on a pedestal occupies the central position of an architectural *capriccio* for which the marble frame was expressly made and of which it is part and parcel. In the picture feigned ruined arches on Composite columns, whose capitals are carved with masks, form a roofless aisle. It must surely be unusual for architecture in a picture to follow so accurately the style of its marble frame. The capitals in the picture are tied by metal rods. A tree, half dead and half sprouting foliage, forms a canopy over the Baptist's head. Under a high sky an idyllic landscape is glimpsed low down in the distance. Little wild flowers like ragged robin sprout from the cracked paving; ivy falls from the drum of the partly demolished dome. The background and foreground detail is minutely delineated. Amidst this wilderness of stone St John raises his right hand in blessing.

Beyond the third altar a monument to *Count Giralamo Cavazza* (d. 1657) is by Giuseppe Sardi, architect of several Baroque façades in Venice. He came from Rome where his Maddalena church is in the Rococo idiom. The TCI guidebook calls the Cavazza monument 'heavy', without exaggeration. In the fourth chapel it is at first surprising – though why exactly I cannot explain – to find amongst this galaxy of southern painters *The Martyrdom of St Lawrence* by Vandyke. However the artist in this case turns out to be, not Sir Anthony, but Daniel, a contemporary who married a Venetian painter. The picture is not a very good one. Instead of lying complacently on his gridiron the saint is being coaxed by an indifferent torturer and a bearded gentleman to meet his martyrdom. The bearded gentleman is pleading with all his might; but Lawrence is so concerned with the crown of glory being proffered him from above that he has momentarily forgotten what all the fuss is about.

Over the doorway to the Cappella di San Mauro is the first of ten paintings by Tintoretto. For the Madonna dell'Orto was the great painter's parish church. Nearby (Fondamenta dei Mori No. 3399) is La Gotica Casa where he worked and in 1594 died. It is a modest little sixteenth-century house with pointed windows and a balcony appropriate for a working artist. Tintoretto was buried in the Madonna dell'Orto, although the exact site of his grave and those of his children in the first chapel to the right of the high altar is unknown.

As for the painting over the entrance to the Cappella di San Mauro, it was formerly two wings of the outer organ doors of the church. The subject is *The Presentation of the Virgin Mary in the Temple* ('Best seen in the afternoon light', says Hugh Honour). Nothing could be more poignant than the solitary child's slight figure, silhouetted against a brilliant patch of sky as, clutching her long skirt, she climbs the steep flight of steps towards the tall, solemn cleric awaiting her in vestments and mitre. She is separated from her mother and the women and children who point and lean forward to watch the spectacle. Scattered groups of beggars look on, amazed. The fragility and vulnerability of the little girl are emphasized by the obelisk which overtops her. Tintoretto must have been influenced by Titian's great canvas in the Accademia of the same subject, finished fourteen years previously. The attitude of the solitary child is similar although Titian painted her midway up a long flight of steps, as it were momentarily pausing in what the Apocrypha describes as the remarkable pace of a three-year-old which so astonished her beholders. Tintoretto was the first great Renaissance artist to depart from the custom of depicting members of the Holy Family as Roman soldiers in togas and matrons in the *stola*. He depicted them like the ordinary people leading ordinary lives around him. Deft master of light and shadow that he was, he so enriched his colours that when the canvases need to be cleaned they often have the consistency of plum pudding. Gautier saw in his paintings elements wild, savage and tragic; they were unlike the majority of Venetian pictures which are naturally happy, sun-loving and radiant.

The polygonal presbytery apse consists of seven compartments – two windows, a central triptych by Palma il Giovane and two colossal canvases by the youthful Tintoretto. They are *The Last Judgement* and *The Adoration of the Golden Calf.* In his devotion to the church Tintoretto was so anxious to cover the bare walls of the presbytery that he offered his services for both canvases free. The first is really impossible to see. It is, like other vast paintings of this particular subject, a sea of limbs, here seemingly washed by wave after wave upon rocks. The figures of the wicked and good, among whom Tintoretto and his wife feature, are audaciously foreshortened. If cleaned they would reveal strongly contrasting lights and shadows, but they are at present veiled by dirt. The electric light time-button allows only the briefest minute for examination. In *Modern Painters* Ruskin, referring to the boat of the condemned, fairly let himself go in an orgy of horror:

the waters of the firmament gathered into one white, ghastly cataract: the river of the wrath of God, roaring down into the gulf where the world has melted with its fervent heat, choked with the ruin of nations, and the limbs of its corpses tossed out of its whirling, like water-wheels. Bat-like, out of the holes and caverns and shadows of the earth, the bones gather, and the clay heaps heave, rattling and adhering into half-kneaded anatomies, that crawl, and startle, and struggle up among the putrid weeds, with the clay clinging to their clotted hair, and their heavy eyes sealed by the earth-darkness . . .

The meaning of this terrible passage can be sensed rather than discerned in the present condition of the huge picture. In writing it Ruskin is supposed to have had in mind a prospect of the Adriatic breaking through the Lido and overwhelming Venice and its wicked citizens.

The second painting is fortunately easier to see and a finer composition. From a height, wingless angels descend like arrows in flight towards Moses who on Mount Sinai emerges from clouds with arms open to receive the tablets of the law extended to him. Below, the fickle Israelites cluster round the calf, borne on a sort of plinth by stalwart men. Women shower the golden beast with jewels, trinkets and flowers. It was these two pictures which first launched Ruskin on a lifelong love of Tintoret, as he and his contemporaries always termed the artist, leading him to warn his readers that they must 'not hope to derive any pleasure from them without resolute study and then not unless [they were] accustomed to decipher the thoughts in a picture patiently'. This love was not shared by his silly little wife Effie. 'John took me to see two large Tintorets', she wrote to her mother, 'but going in hot to a place like a well to see a death's head crowned with leaves gave me such a shiver that I ran out of the church and I do not intend to return again.'

High up in the left aisle a glazed gallery, like a royal pew, overlooks the presbytery. In the fourth recessed chapel of the left aisle, la Cappella dei Contarini, are six busts of members of that dogal family, the two central ones by Vittoria. The one of *Cardinal Gaspare Contarini* (d.1542) is a youthful work under the influence of Sansovino; the other, of *Procurator Tommaso Contarini* (d.1578), a work of the sculptor's full maturity. On the altar Tintoretto's *St Agnes resuscitating the son of a Roman prefect* is painted in warm tones of chiaroscuro. In the Cappella Morisini are two canvases by Domenico, the great Iacopo's son. In the first chapel, that is to say the one nearest the west end and facing the Conegliano *Baptist*, is the beautiful little *Madonna and Child* painted by Giovanni Bellini at the age of twenty-one when he was still under the influence of Mantegna. The Child, who has evidently seen something untoward, is about to bellow. The Mother, while grasping him firmly with large peasant fingers, is paying no heed to these incarnate manifestations and contemplating the eternal verities instead.

SAN NICOLÒ DEI MENDICOLI

Twelfth to sixteenth centuries

From wherever you are staying the little church of St Nicholas of the Beggars is likely to be at the end of a long walk. It stands at the extreme western end of the Dorsoduro, beyond the Stazione Maritima in a poor out-of-the-way quarter on a small peninsula formed by a three-sided junction of canals. Until very lately the surrounding houses were exclusively lived in by fishermen, dockhands and artisans.

San Nicolò dei Mendicoli is one of the most ancient ecclesiastical foundations of Venice. Although originally built in the late seventh century it has been so often and so much altered throughout the centuries that at first I found difficulty in deciding to which period the present building chiefly belonged. Yet although the character and flavour of the interior are predominantly *cinquecento* there is something about the church that is different from any other in Venice. It is timeless. It is homely. It is almost like a simple English country church which contains unexpected treasures.

The west entrance façade of the church is curiously truncated in that Venetian manner by a little *canonica*, or priest's house, which abuts upon the southern half, cutting right through the middle of the pent roof of the atrium. This atrium is basically fourteenth-century and in medieval times was a dwelling place for poor religious women (*le pinzocchere*). Four square stone piers carry fretted wooden beams on which the sloping roof rests. Sturdy grilles of wrought iron between the piers have been carefully contrived to curve and bulge over the capitals. The nave façade has a large central eye-window of Istrian stone between a pair of long rectangular windows. Over the eye-window are the remains of a small bifurcated window with primitive capital dating from the twelfth century. Attached to the little projecting house in which the priest dwells rises a stumpy campanile, composed of the usual late twelfth- century *lesene*, but lacking a crowning feature. This was apparently knocked off by a German shell in the last war. Below the triple round-headed openings of the belfry is fixed a clock of which the hands, like the desiccated limbs of an old starfish, no longer function. A stone tablet records in Latin words so abbreviated that one can only deduce something about the hours fleeing like memory and life itself.

If you pass behind the campanile you come to a rather squalid *campo* on to which the front door of the *canonica* opens. It is crawling with mangy cats greedily gobbling up the handfuls of dry bread thrown to them by compassionate residents. Over the high wall of a back garden two grey monkeys aimlessly chase each other round and round a small wire cage. This *campo* is bounded on its west and south sides by the Rio San Nicolò.

The side entrance to the north aisle of the church faces the tiny Campo San Nicolò. This *campo* is paved and has in its centre the inevitable well-head, now disused, with heavy metal lid clamped down in order to prevent any of those superfluous children falling into it. A white Istrian stone column carries a small wingless lion of St Mark holding the Gospel in its paws. The lion has a bewildered expression on its worn face as though asking, 'What should I do next?' On the edge of the Rio di Terese a pole rises from a stone socket on which is recorded the perennial gratitude for blessings, bestowed by the 'Republic' on the Nicolotti and their 'Doge', of his grateful nephews, together with the good wishes of the municipality. To this strange effusion is attached the seemingly odd date, 1876.

The Nicolotti, inhabitants of this district, have since time immemorial regarded themselves almost as a race apart from the rest of Venice. In fact, since they colonized the area long before the Venetians decided to establish themselves perman- ently on the Rivo Alto, they well may be. For centuries they were one of two rival factions, the other being the Castellani, inhabitants of the extreme east end of Venice, like the

Montagues and Capulets. The Nicolotti had their own banner, depicting column and winged lion, and their own so-called doge, or head fisherman, who under the superintendence of a member of the Signoria was elected by the community. To him the community were extremely loyal. To their neighbour communities they were intensely provocative. Between the months of September and December the Nicolotti engaged in regular fist-fights with the Castellani. The encounters took place on the Ponte dei Pugni off the Campo San Barnabà, which then had no parapets (as shown in a drawing by Ruskin) so that the combatants might hurl their adversaries into the water without unduly hurting them. Footprints on the bridge in white marble are a reminder of the rules. In 1705 however the '*guerra dei Pugni*' turned into so sanguinary a battle, in which stones and knives were used, that several combatants were maimed and even killed. In consequence future encounters were forbidden by the Republic. Instead rivalry was confined to the *Forze d'Ercole*, acrobatic competitions in which pyramids of athletes were formed, the highest being acclaimed as victors, or to harmless regatta races.

Today the Nicolotti seem to be friendly and jolly people. One autumn afternoon my wife and I sat on the bridge which joins the Fondamenta Bari to the Campo San Nicolò, watching the coming and going to a local wedding in the church. After the newly-married couple emerged through the west door and the usual family groups had been snapped by a dozen amateur photographers, a crowd of Nicolotti, assembled like ourselves to enjoy the spectacle and the fun, suddenly poured into the nave. Within seconds out they came, their arms filled with bunches of arum lilies and sheaves of gladioli with which the bride's family had doubtless at great expense embellished the interior. They were blatantly looting as much as they could carry, one ancient woman staggering under a plastic pot of aspidistra, but in the most open, good-tempered manner, amidst shouts of triumphant laughter.

Facing the north entrance of the church a handsome descent of six white curved steps down to the Rio di Terese was constructed to lead the 'Doge of the Nicolotti', clothed in a threadbare woollen garment of scarlet and wearing a peruque and 'a gentleman's cap' (*berretto da gentiluomo*) on the day following his election, into a gondola. Thence he was conveyed to the Ducal Palace to receive a welcoming embrace from his brother doge. The handsome north entrance consists of a frontispiece of white Istrian stone (seventeenth century) against a dull brick background. On the apex of a swan-neck pediment are carved the words, '*Signum Filii Hominis Anno* 1771'. On either side of the portal a niche contains a figure, that on the right headless and that on the left holding the crucified Christ; above the door the Assumption (*Assunta*).

The plan of the interior is nave, two aisles, transept, apsidal presbytery and two lateral chapels, deeply recessed like caverns. In other words a basilica in miniature. But at first all one sees is a crepuscular twinkling of oil lamps and candles. Of an afternoon the church is usually empty save for the silent presence of the old priest who tends it with the utmost love and care. He is either praying in a side chapel or softly pacing the red and white chequered floor. The inside is extremely rich – a nice contrast to the poverty of the district which the church serves. One must always remember that since Latin churches were the people's palaces as well as places of prayer they were, particularly during the Tridentine centuries, gloriously gilded and colourful. Wealthy benefactors endowed them with the richest and rarest adornments which, far from resenting, the poor, who always crave glamour, relished and cherished as their own communal possessions. It is a modern and mistaken premise, dear to democratic Protestants, that because the dwellings of the Third World may be deprived of refrigerators and television sets therefore it is wicked to allow the houses of God in the West to remain beautiful.

The stalwart columns supporting nave and aisles are fourteenth-century; the Ionic parcel-gilt capitals of the two last columns on the left bear the dates 1361 and 1364 respectively. Around 1580 the nave was transformed. The arches were wainscoted and the clerestorys divided into large panels by fluted wooden pilasters. The panels of the north clerestory were filled with paintings of episodes in the life of Christ by Alvise

Dal Friso, a sixteenth-century disciple of Veronese by no means rivalling that great courtly luminary.

> Our painter was his pupil by repute,
> His match if not his master absolute

as Browning put it in under-statement. Of the scenes on the south clerestory four – *Christ presented to Herod, The Flagellation, Christ and St Veronica* and *The Crucifixion* – are from the workshops of Veronese, and one, *The Resurrection*, is by Palma il Giovane.

The flat nave ceiling is divided into panels, the central roundel of *St Nicholas in Glory* being by Francesco Montemezzano, a portrait painter from Verona. Among the surrounding panels St Nicholas is depicted felling a tree which some ill-advised pagans had been adoring, and rescuing sailors in a tempest. The extraordinary richness of the newly cleaned paintings is enhanced by the gilded statues of the *Apostles* standing on brackets over the pilasters of both clerestorys and the top-heavy mask heads on the keystones of the arches. The architectural concept is continued across the rood screen (above the presbytery arch) from which rises the carved *Crucified Christ* between the Madonna, St John and two angels. Thus three sides of the rectangular nave are unbroken, the fourth or west end carrying organ pipes within a Palladian tabernacle. The sumptuous organ gallery is adorned with three lively canvases of *The Miracle of St Martha* by Carletto Caliari (late sixteenth century). This artist, who was one of Veronese's sons, painted many of the ceiling panels. Four over-size consoles support the loft.

The second chapel in the south aisle exhibits the grisly corpse of St Nicholas, though which St Nicholas no one seems able to explain. St Nicholas of Bari, the most famous of the name, who was imprisoned by Diocletian and condemned Arianism at the Council of Nicea, was Bishop of Myra in Asia Minor. When the Saracens overran Myra in the eleventh century his miracle-working bones were removed to Bari in Apulia where they still repose, exuding a sweet-scented myrrh, called 'the manna of St Nicholas', that contains health-giving properties. His renown is world-wide and in Russia he is so exalted that until the Revolution it was believed that he would replace God when God became too old. In America he became the original Santa Claus, the provider of children's gifts, and throughout the world he has always been the protector of sailors and fishermen. Hence the fact that the little church of the mendicants on Venice's Dorsoduro was dedicated to him in the twelfth century.

But these particulars do not identify St Nicholas of Bari with his namesake lying inside a glazed sarcophagus, with black scowling face, a silver and gold cap awry on his head which rests on a plush cushion, a black emaciated hand grasping a withered stalk, and feet of the same dusky hue tied to pointed sandals protruding from a yellow robe. The third chapel of the sacrament and baptistery combined was re-fashioned in the eighteenth century. It has an enchanting balustrade formed of a brocaded stuff hanging in folds, with fringes and tassels, all of white marble. The chapel dome has Rococo plaster panels filled with frescoes on a pale green ground.

The most ancient part of the interior to survive is the twelfth-century presbytery apse with Byzantine cornice. The semi-dome is perforated with frescoed panels, the *Gloria* painted by Alvise Dal Friso. Behind the high altar and within a niche the effigy in painted wood of St Nicholas is in the act of blessing. He has a powerful, bearded face, and his lips are open as though uttering the benediction. Three gold balls are balanced on his left knee. The effigy came from the workshop of the Buon family in the middle of the fifteenth century and is well worth the risk of trespassing on forbidden territory to see. As Henry James put it:

> many a masterpiece lurks in the unaccommodating gloom of side chapels and sacristies. Many a noble work is perched behind the duty candles and muslin roses of a scantily-visited altar; some of them, indeed, are hidden behind the altar, in a darkness that can never be explored. The facilities offered you are of a kind of mockery of your irritated desire. You stand on tip-toe on a three-legged stool, you climb a ricketty ladder, you almost mount upon the shoulders of the *custode*.

A picture of the stout and venerable novelist enacting the last acrobatic feat is indeed curious. In the chapel to the left of the presbytery the perspective relief of two angels in adoration is an eighteenth-century adaptation of a Lombardesque design.

With the fall of the Republic in 1797 the fortunes of San Nicolò dei Mendicoli declined. The French suppressed the chapter and its assets were sequestrated. In 1807 the church was partially closed. Then in 1810 the parish was done away with. The church suffered further loss of pictures and treasures by sale. It was regarded as a write-off. In his guide to Venice (1884) Augustus Hare made no mention of it as though it did not exist. In 1900 it was kept completely closed and left to rot. In 1903 restoration of a sort was put in hand. Until San Nicolò was re-opened in 1924 many more treasures were stolen. The British Venice in Peril Fund has recently adopted it and restored it to the flourishing condition in which you may see it today.

CASA OR CA' D'ORO

1421–40

The Ca' d'Oro is in a way the most famous palace in Venice if we exclude the Doges' Palace, which like Buckingham Palace is that of a head of state. It is certainly the most architecturally flamboyant. Throughout the nineteenth century, in fact since Ruskin raved and wrote about it in the 1840s, and well into the present century it continued to enjoy the zenith of its popularity. Cultivated people regarded it as the most beautiful of Venetian domestic buildings. Its extraordinary reputation indicates the authority which Ruskin exercised upon the consciousness of architectural connoisseurs in England and on the continent (Proust is an example among the French) for more than a century. Not until the 1940s did anyone with pretensions to sound judgement of architecture dare to dispute the great panjandrum's dictation on matters Venetian, even long after love of the English Gothic revival had gone into eclipse.

It is highly doubtful whether the Ca' d'Oro, or for that matter any other Gothic palace, is anyone's favourite Venetian palace today, which is not saying that *anyone* is necessarily right. In our age of stark simplicity, not to say puritanism of architecture, we have grown to dislike in domestic buildings the fussiness, the plethora of decorative detail, the ecclesiastical gloom of superfluous ogees, crockets, cusps, gargoyles, pinnacles, finials and general frowstiness which we associate with Victorian rectories.

Yet as the name of our Venetian palace implies, frowstiness cannot have been applicable when the building was first erected. It was on the contrary quite shockingly colourful in a merry-go-round sort of way. Whatever readers of this book may now think, the Ca' d'Oro is still a textbook building of cosmopolitan fame. Moreover it is one of the few, very few palaces which the public may see inside. Even so, alas, owing to the misfortunes that have dogged the structure since Ruskin first proclaimed its eminence, very little of the interior remains. These misfortunes moreover have been largely due to its very eminence, for which Ruskin cannot be held responsible. Its mangling and mauling by admirers was actually taking place before Ruskin appeared on the Venetian horizon.

Venice is chock-a-block with Byzantine, Gothic and early Renaissance palaces along the Grand Canal and down the narrowest *rii*. All the passer-by is vouchsafed is a glimpse of the façade, usually with shuttered windows, a cluster of decaying striped *pali* and the slippery, weed-strewn steps of a water-gate against which no gondola has for twenty, thirty, or forty years scraped its black flanks. One cannot imagine what *Aspern Papers* scenes are enacted within the darkened rooms of the mezzanines, for the first floors are mostly occupied by offices, judging by the strips of neon lights screwed to beamed ceilings. Byzantine, Gothic or early Renaissance, the palaces date from the late thirteenth century to the end of the fifteenth, and beyond the shape of the window heads, rounded, shouldered or ogival, they display little difference of form. With the full Renaissance and the Baroque comes a distinctive classical change. The palaces of these later eras are fewer.

Whereas the old Byzantine palace fronts, like the Palazzo Loredan and Palazzo Farsetti at the Rialto, had long continuous arcades from end to end round a central courtyard, the Gothic palace fronts are inclined to break into a central group of arcades, lighting the first-floor saloon (the *portego*) only, and to be flanked by isolated single windows of lesser rooms. The Palazzo Bernardo and Palazzo Foscari fronts are disposed in this way. The Ca' d'Oro is different. But first of all let us consider the builder of this palace.

Marino Contarini, a rich patrician, member of a family of eight doges of the name and a procurator of St Mark's, began building in 1421. The façade was all but finished ten years later when Marino was negotiating the purchase of coloured marbles for the final embellishments. By 1440 the entire palace was finished. Marino kept a daily journal and left accounts in minute detail of the work as it progressed. From these accounts it appears that he was largely his own architect, with the assistance of Marco d'Amadeo, a master builder, and Matteo Reverti, a master builder and sculptor, both Milanese, the latter being of higher standing in that he had carved some important figures on the dome of Milan Cathedral. They were soon joined by Giovanni Buon and his son Bartolomeo. Sir John Pope-Hennessy tells us that after work on the Madonna dell'Orto the Buons' next recorded activities were at the Ca' d'Oro in 1422.

Although sprung from Bergamo the Buon became completely Venetian. Exactly how much and what detail of the Ca' d'Oro can be attributed to the Buon father and son is still uncertain. But the dynasty was henceforth to play a considerable part in the flowering of the Venetian style during the transitional period from the flamboyant Gothic to the early Renaissance. Bartolomeo, Giovanni's son, was between 1439 and 1443 to construct the Porta della Carta on the north-west front of the Ducal Palace (he inserted his name on the lintel) and to establish a large workshop in which he and his family were to function until the beginning of the sixteenth century. At all events owing to jealousy, relations between the Milanese Reverti and the Venetian Buon were strained throughout the building of the Ca' d'Oro. Other artists in large numbers were called upon by Procurator Contarini to collaborate in producing the masterpiece. Documents reveal how Contarini directed his men to copy windows and capitals of palaces he admired, notably the Palazzo Priuli at San Severo.

Conservative though Marino Contarini undoubtedly was in building a Gothic palace at a time when other rich men were adopting the Lombardic style, yet he was original in respect of the façade, the most romantic in Europe according to Henry James. No other in Venice had or has been so highly decorated, or is so markedly idiosyncratic in its detail, not to mention quality. But the most unusual thing about it is its being off balance. One might suppose that the *portego* and second-floor colonnades of six openings flanked by close single windows of entirely different design, with balconies (incidentally all balconies are missing in Ruskin's incomplete drawing of 1845) and the five water-gate openings, were meant to comprise the complete palace and that the right-hand section was a later addition. But this was not so. The entire façade as it stands was what Contarini intended. The predominating plain wall surface of the right-hand section, pierced only by one square window on each floor to serve the family's private apartments, is highly successful in affording some relief from the extreme ornamentation of the greater part of the façade.

The very obvious influence of the Doges' Palace upon the first-floor arcade is evident in shapes and patterns from the filigree heads down to the balustrades between the columns. The Doges' Palace arcade dating from the first decade of the fifteenth century makes it at least ten years older than the Ca' d'Oro counterpart. The Ca' d'Oro arcade gives on to no central court but forms an open loggia to the long *portego*. As Thomas Coryate remarked in 1611, every old palace had in the middle of the façade, 'a little beneath the top of the fronte', a pleasant terrace and balconies, not only to give grace but to afford 'a delectable prospect' in the cool of the evening. The arcading of the *piano nobile* was therefore very important here because the *portego* is chiefly lit from the Canal end, glazed windows at the far rear end admitting only a modicum of light. The second-floor arcading, which is a lower and modified version, beautifully conforms to that of the *piano nobile*.

The ground, or rather water-floor arcade of four pointed openings and one central, wider and round-headed opening, was designed to admit gondolas into the palace. So wafer-thin is the slither of stone on which the feet of the palace rest that it is difficult to tell what is rippling water and what Istrian pavement. One is reminded of Proust's description of a gondola waiting outside a palace, 'shaken as though upon the crest of a blue wave, by the thrust of a flashing, prancing water, which took alarm on finding itself pent between the dancing boat and the slapping marble'. Behind the water-gate the ground floor, being extremely damp, is uninhabitable.

A further influence of the Doges' Palace is found on the elaborate cresting of the roof parapet. This is not crenellation or battlements but, in Ruskin's words, 'adaptations of the light and crown-like ornaments which crest the walls of the Arabian mosques'. The fall of the cresting from the extremities of the parapet and its rise to the centre give that barely perceptible movement which the minutely convex podium of the Parthenon does to that miraculous monument. Seen from the Grand Canal the skyline contour is fairy-like.

Being so delicate, the parapet suffered serious injury in the great earthquake of 1511 and both then and subsequently had to be repaired. The slender, cable-like colonnettes of three strands imposed upon the angles of the façade are evidence of the need to reduce the apparent weight of the building carried by the piles. Single strands in the same motif are carved as string courses and frames to the panels of the right-hand section; also above the windows as little roundels enclosing balls the size of cricket balls on pins so as to cast shadows in the slanting sunshine. Similar balls feature on the parapet cresting. The carved decoration of the façade is attributed to the Buon father and son. In 1431 Marino Contarini commissioned a painter to pick out the stone relief carving in ultramarine, red and gold.

The palace is easily approached today by the *vaporetto* which has a station (called Ca' d'Oro) moored to a wooden bridge at the right corner of the façade. You step straight from the boat up the narrow Calle della Ca' d'Oro along the return side of the palace. The wall of this side is of stark and unadorned brick except for a fine arched gateway with terracotta cresting which gives access to the principal courtyard. This, the proper land entrance, is not at present used and admission to the public is by a doorway and modern ticket office at the rear of the building. But the gateway has a lunette carved with rampant foliage and splendid armorial bearings of the Contarini in marble, the work of Nicolo Romanello. The angel holding the shield within the arch is by Matteo Reverti, and the wooden doors are made up from fragments of the original.

In the middle of the great courtyard, on a square block

slightly raised above the herring-bone brick pavement, stands a well-head (*la vera da pozzo*) which was carved by Bartolomeo Buon in red Verona marble. It is this sculptor's masterpiece, decorated with allegorical figures of Strength, Justice and Charity seated on lions among dense Gothic foliage. Through a screen of four widely spaced columns supporting the glazed section of the *portego*, a long and dark hall, or *portico terreno*, stretches its immense length towards the water-gate on the Grand Canal. The floor is paved with colourful inlay of polychrome marbles, and the walls are clad in tiles of grey and red marble. Antique columns, partly of Greek marble, with Romanesque and Byzantine capitals carry a wooden ceiling composed of little panels, recently restored. Fragments of antique sculpture are scattered in the *portico terreno*.

Returning to the large courtyard you mount the *quattrocento* staircase to reach the *portego* on the *piano nobile*. Once covered with a wooden roof in the usual Venetian fashion, the return flight of the stairs is supported by pointed arches against the west wall. The balusters, handrail, steps and tread ends were carved by Matteo Reverti and his masons. A series of small busts and one heraldic lion adorn the newel posts.

I have already mentioned that the Ca' d'Oro, and especially its interior underwent many unfortunate vicissitudes. The Contarini family did not own the place beyond the fifteenth century. The marriage of Marino's granddaughter to Pietro Marcello in 1484 brought it into the possession of her husband's descendants. When the Marcello family parted with it in the early seventeenth century others owned it for short periods. After the fall of the Republic it changed hands several times. When Ruskin first saw it in 1845 it had for two years been the property of the Russian Prince Alexander Troubetskoi. He bought it for his mistress, Maria Taglioni, a well-known Italian ballet dancer already married to the French Comte de Voisins. Badly formed and plain of feature, Taglioni danced with admirable grace, her great triumph being the creation of *La Sylphide* in 1832 which marked the apex of romantic ballet dancing. She is said to have been the first to introduce *sur les pointes* dancing. She was some ten years older than her lover, and the liaison eventually ended in Troubetskoi marrying Maria's daughter. Before this happened however Taglioni lost no time in ruining the Ca' d'Oro by making the most fundamental alterations inside and out.

Not only did Maria engage an architect to redecorate the palace to her own excruciating taste but she dismantled the glorious exterior staircase, selling the marble piece-meal to a house-breaker. She also sold Buon's well-head from the courtyard. Ruskin witnessed the beautiful slabs of red marble carved in noble spiral mouldings which formed the bases of the balconies being dashed to pieces by the workmen. It was during these appalling depredations that he drew the façade balcony-less. Of what was left he later recorded that the capitals of the windows in the upper storey were of the finest Gothic carving, made to look like clusters of natural leaves, whereas the restorers' copies were like clumsy masses of kneaded dough with finger holes in them. He wrote to his father on 23 September 1845:

> You cannot imagine what an unhappy day I spent yesterday before the Casa d'Oro, vainly attempting to draw it while the workmen were hammering it down before my face. It would have put me to my hardest possible shifts at any rate, for it is intolerably difficult, and the intricacy and colour of it as a study of colour inconceivable . . . but fancy trying to work while one sees the cursed plasterers hauling up beams and dashing in the old walls and shattering the mouldings, and pulling barges across your gondola bows and driving you here and there, up and down and across, and all the while with the sense that *now* one's art is not enough to be of the slightest service, but that in ten years more one might have done some glorious things.

The lamentable destruction and restoration taking place under his eyes drove him nearly mad with misery and frustration. So badly did he take it that he could not finish the coloured drawing of the front and left the right section in outline.

Needless to say Taglioni's residence at the Ca' d'Oro was of short duration. Like so many artistes of the kind, her fortunes veered sharply from poverty to wealth and back to poverty again. She ended her career teaching deportment to Queen Victoria's children. The Ca' d'Oro passed through further hands, a Jewish family owning it in the late 1860s. Then it was divided into apartments. Finally in 1894 it was bought by Baron Giorgio Franchetti. The Baron was not only immensely rich but a man of artistic discernment and enthusiasm. He made it his life's task to restore the palace outwardly and inwardly to what he believed it originally to have been. He put back the demolished balconies and retrieved much of the carved decoration of the façade. He managed to buy the mutilated staircase remains, fitting the marble pieces together and re-carving the tread-ends where necessary. He purchased the famous well-head and put it back where it belonged in the courtyard. Henri de Régnier came upon the Baron one day on hands and knees on the mosaic pavement of the *portico terreno*, carefully fitting into the empty holes little *tesserae* of coloured marbles exactly matching those lost, with admirable patience and minute concentration.

The Baron, like many connoisseurs of his time, furnished the Ca' d'Oro with sumptuous Renaissance walnut furniture and tapestries which he placed against and hung upon heavily brocaded and wine-red brocatelle walls. He collected busts by Vittoria, reliefs by the Lombardi and Sansovino, painted *cassoni* and some splendid Renaissance bronzes. He collected paintings by Carpaccio and Mantegna (St Sebastian transfixed by more arrows than any ordinary mortal could remain upright under) and the followers of numerous old masters, not always as authentic as they should be. The Baron gave the palace and collections to the municipality of Venice in 1916, continuing until his death in 1922 to improve the building and add to the collections while living in a floor of an adjacent palace. For a long time the council neglected the munificent bequest and the wishes of the generous benefactor. Only lately has the Galleria Franchetti been taken in hand. Today the treasures are displayed in what is a totally modern museum, fitted with the most up-to-date strip lighting and glass partitions. Hardly a trace is left of the Gothic-Renaissance residence which Baron Franchetti had contrived at great expense and with loving care.

When all is said and done it is the façade of the Ca' d'Oro which enlists our interest and captures our imagination. View it from, say, the Rialto fish market a little downstream on the opposite shore. The longer one looks the more evanescent it becomes. No other palace floats quite so lightly on the Grand Canal. The tight crochet-work arcades of the *piano nobile* and upper floor unravel themselves into gossamer when twilight or an evening mist descends upon the Lagoon. Morning, midday or afternoon the reflection of the façade is never still in the water. When the sun is actually setting the water is broken into a thousand fragments of every colour of the spectrum, which Canaletto and Bellotto could not convincingly capture but which one finds refracted in the Venetian scenes of Monet. But as far as I know the French Impressionists did not care to paint in Venice. When the Ca' d'Oro really was the Golden Palace what the shifting water must have made of the reflection is almost too disturbing to contemplate. Turner alone, one feels, would have faced up to it in a haze of glory. I have stood on the *portego* by moonlight when it stencilled the filigree shadows of columns, capitals, trefoils and quatrefoils on the bare floor so sharply that my own inescapable silhouette was an affront, as it were, to the pure architectural outline in which Baron Franchetti's substitute details were softened and those of Marco d'Amadeo, Matteo de Reverti and the Buons momentarily brought back to life, that life which stone no less than the flesh of creatures enjoys.

SANTA MARIA DEI MIRACOLI

1481 – 89

'A jewel of a church', Robert Browning called it. He was not the last admirer to compare it to a gem. Lorenzetti refers to it as, '*Questo prezioso gioello del Rinascimento.*' James Morris writes, 'No little building in the world is more fascinating than the Renaissance church of Santa Maria dei Miracoli, hidden away behind the Rialto like a precious stone in ruffled satin'. I am not so sure about the ruffled satin because the water of the little canal that flanks one side of it is static. 'One of the most beautiful small buildings in the world', Hugh Honour has reiterated. He also sees it like one of those temples in a Bellini painting, which indeed it resembles. Closer still would the resemblance be were it sited in open landscape with blue foothills in the distance, ruinous with saplings thrusting apart the crumbling masonry and little wild flowers sprouting from the crevices in a paved foreground. As it is, Santa Maria dei Miracoli no more knows the country than Carpaccio did. This essentially Venetian church closely approximates in my opinion to the stark urbanity of Carpaccio's temples found in the background of, for instance, *The Return of the Ambassadors* and *The Departure of the Pilgrims* of the St Ursula series in the Accademia, begun the year after the Miracoli church was finished. Another even closer approximation is to this Venetian artist's church in the background of *The Visitation*. Carpaccio's buildings are so complete, by which I mean so much of a piece, so utterly contemporary, also so meticulous and holy, that one can scarcely imagine people daring to enter for fear of defiling them. They resemble not so much buildings, or even jewellery, as caskets for jewellery. You have merely to open the lid, look inside and extract one by one the treasures they contain. And this impression of an outsize casket is what you get if, in walking from the Rialto down tortuous passages which skirt the Teatro Malibran, a route impossible to describe and even to follow by map, but which in the end, if you are lucky, will project you from the Calle dei Miracoli on to a bridge over a *rio* of that name. There immediately on your left, rising sheer out of the water, is the church you have desperately been searching.

Santa Maria dei Miracoli is unlike the majority of Venetian churches in that it did not grow from foundations of previous sanctuaries on a site dating from the dark ages. Nor has it ever been altered since first built. It is entirely and absolutely of its decade, the 1480s. This does not mean that it was not intended to be a small votive chapel which changed into a church when money was found in the course of building to be pouring in from contributors. The reason for its creation is simple. A rich merchant called Francesco Amadi (you pass his Gothic palace in the Corte Nuova before diving into the interstices around the Teatro Malibran) commissioned a painting of the Madonna for the corner of his palace in 1409. He paid the artist, one Nicolò di Pietro less than two ducats for it. By 1477 it had become an object of profound veneration. It has always been a mystery to me how an old picture first acquired the reputation of being miracle-working, or the product of St Luke, patron of all Christian painters. Did some freak of sunlight once make the eyes of the Madonna twinkle? Did some leper in passing it by become instantaneously healed? Did some holy man solemnly aver that he recognized the brush strokes of the Evangelist: and if so, how did he persuade contemporaries to believe him? The credulity of medieval people was contagious. The power of self-deception was commensurate with implicit integrity as well as faith. In the particular case of the Madonna dei Miracoli, an old woman, outrageously stabbed and left for dead on 23 August 1480 – the very date is known – was cured by sympathizers' intercession to the icon which everyone knew had been painted and paid for a mere seventy-two years previously. There was no mystery. There was merely well proven and swiftly accrued sanctity attached to the icon.

In fact so great were the crowds assembled to venerate the icon by day and night that Francesco Amadi's nephew and heir, Angelo, felt moved to hang it on the palace of his neighbours, the Barozzi family. It was indeed a questionable honour to confer unsolicited. The Barozzi became fed up with the inconvenience; and litigation between the two families was threatened. An ugly issue was avoided by an ingenious solution on the part of Angelo. By dint of soliciting alms and providing a sum from his own coffers he decided to build a chapel in which to enshrine the family Madonna. Without delay he commissioned the architect Pietro Lombardo, aided by his sons Tullio and Antonio, and the numerous stone and marble masons from Pietro's workshop to set to work. On 31 December 1489 the miracle-working icon was solemnly transported by night and installed on the brand new high altar.

Pietro Lombardo (*c.* 1438 – 1515) whose name has appeared already in these pages, was not Venetian born but as the name implies came, although he was a native of the Ticino in Switzerland, from Lombardy. Nevertheless his arrival in Venice in 1474 introduced to the Renaissance a style distinguished above all by façades encrusted with slabs, discs and panels of precious marble inlay. Pietro was the father of several sons – Tullio (1460 – 1532) is the most renowned – who all worked in the family yard. It is not always known what part was played by Antonio (*c.* 1458–*c.* 1516), Giulio and Tullio's son Sante, for the whole Lombardi clan were equally skilled in architecture, sculpture and marble inlay. Besides they nearly always worked together. But generally speaking, the father Pietro's sculpture is the most virile, Tullio's the most lyrical and Antonio's more closely related to painting and nature. Among the buildings attributed to them are the Procuratie Vecchie in the Piazza and the enchanting Palazzo Dario on the Grand Canal, its toppling façade richly inlaid with roundels of porphyry and *verde antico*. The Lombardi gave their name to a great number of monuments, notably in the Frari and San Zanipolo churches, monuments displaying unmistakable sculptural qualities of fastidiousness, dignity and classical eclecticism. The jumble of ingredients, winged *putti*, dolphins, vases, candelabra, honeysuckles and armorial shields, is often ill-assorted and at times indigestible. One sometimes regrets that the sculptor has been too zealous in his endeavours. As Jean Cocteau put it, '*Il y a quelque chose de fou et de profondément honnête dans ce décor*'. The honesty cannot be overlooked.

The casket-like appearance of Santa Maria dei Miracoli is from nowhere more apparent than from the bridge by which we have approached it, for from that stance we view it from a height. What we see is the west end with its hemispherical lunette, and in perspective the north side receding in sharp perspective over the water of the *rio* we are in process of crossing.

All four of the church's elevations are clad in marble. Thomas Coryate, who like so many travellers deemed it the fairest of all the churches he came upon, seemed to notice only the milk-whiteness of the walls. Milk-white, certainly, with a skim of violet veining, the ground of the walls, or more properly the fields of the panels of which they are composed, being in *pavonazetto* marble, fabled to be stained by the blood of Atys. This marble was beloved by the imperial Romans because of its semi-transparency. It was not quarried in Italy but in Greece. However the components – pilasters, window surrounds, portals, not to mention the purely decorative adjuncts, are in a variety of richest and rarest marbles, brought, tradition has it, from discarded remnants of the Byzantine spoil left unused by the masons working on St Mark's. They consist of slabs and veneers of *brocotello rosso*, a shell-like confection, blood red Verona, purple porphyry, *verdè antico* and lemon-yellow serpentine. Moreover each of the four sides of the church is decorated in a different shade of colour, the west end in deep porphyry, the north and south sides in light red and yellow, and the east end in shades of blue and grey. The architectural purist will pounce upon Pietro's solecism in making the lower order Corinthian and the upper Ionic. Strictly speaking they should be the other way round but Pietro preferred to put the more decorative order where it could easily be seen from eye level, and be blowed to the rigid rules of antiquity.

The four fronts are then of two orders, the lower forming a sort of blind arcade under a flat architrave and the upper, which is the higher of the two, a blind loggia of arches. The projecting cornices of both cast dark shadows across the luminous walls. The immense semi-circular tympanum of the west end, indicating the shape of the barrel roof it supports, is disproportionately heavy, reminding me of the lids of those domed tin trunks which at the beginning of this century were for some reason used exclusively by domestic servants and to be seen hoisted by a posse of porters into a guard's van at railway stations. This crowning feature is made more aggressive by a vast rose window round which revolve lesser apertures and two satellites of multi-coloured marbles.

The north or canal side is best seen from the Campo Santa Maria dei Miracoli which is approached from the far end of the church. This means passing by the south side and east end, the bases of which are protected by iron posts and rails. On a jamb of the door of the south side note a small medallion relief of *The Baptism of Christ*, very delicately carved. Someone has cut the date of 1655 beside it. Indeed on all four sides roundels and on the spandrels of the upper stage angels and prophets and saints are carved by the Lombardi family. Over the west door the *Madonna and Child* has the signature Pirgotele, a Greek pseudonym signifying Giorgio Lascaris, a foreign member of the Lombardo workshop.

Adrian Stokes remarked that the absence of a raised footway over the wide space on the south front of the church has allowed, like the water on the north side, an unbroken horizontal plane from which the building grows. This parity of levels caused him to observe the church – no longer the little jewel casket once you are close to it – like a grand vessel detached from its surroundings. On reaching the bridge over the wide *rio* by which the *campo* is approached you must stop in order to view the oblique north front, as well as the east end, from this vantage point. From here the church really does, with a little imagination, become a vessel riding the canal, the plinths which support the row of pilasters of the north side just above the water level seeming, in Stokes's words, 'to float away from us in perfect line as might a flotilla of swans'. The Miracoli is the only church in Venice actually springing from a canal. And springing is what the church is doing, being 'thrust upwards' from both pavement and water by the unusually prominent moulded base.

The movement implied by Stokes as of a ship escorted by swans was deliberately contrived by Pietro Lombardo. Wishing to make the church look larger than it could possibly be on a restricted site he resorted to 'optical illusions'. Hugh Honour describes how Pietro pushed the windows on both stages of the long north front to the sides instead of the middle of the arcades so as to make them, viewed from the *campo* bridge, look recessed, and to feign greater 'depth to the flat surface' and greater length to the nave than is the case. This well-known trick of perspective is more usual in Baroque than Renaissance architecture.

The east annexe comprising the presbytery has some curious idiosyncrasies. There are two windows in the three arcades of the upper stage. Each is set, not in the middle of the first and third arcade as might be expected, but at the inner side. The effect contrived is that of a face with a squint. The explanation is revealed by an inspection of the inside of the presbytery. There the same windows are touching the walls and could not possibly be set further apart. The semi-octagonal campanile is so jambed against the north wall of the presbytery that it cuts into the eye window of the tympanum, and the belfry is squashed into the dome. Then the ground space between the campanile and the end of the church is paved in a slope to resemble a steep bank over the canal as though to prevent people from trespassing there and falling into the water. In the head of the central (blind) arcade of the upper stage a tiny but beautiful bust of a saint with seraphic expression has been placed rather incongruously. He holds his right hand to his cheek.

The interior of the Miracoli church is as dazzling as the exterior. The walls of the aisle-less nave and the pavement are likewise encrusted with polychrome marbles. As on the exterior the nave walls are divided into two stages by a cornice. Grey, green and yellow panels are framed with red uprights and horizontals. The barrel roof is formed of wooden panels in rectangles, diamonds and squares, some parti-gilt. They contain fifty paintings of the heads of Old Testament prophets and patriarchs, the work of Pier Maria Pennacchi and others in 1528 – a waste, one would suppose, of the artists' efforts because from the ground the subjects are quite indistinguishable, although the colours are very effective.

You enter the church under a gallery and low ceiling which contains a central panel of the *Madonna and Child* by Palma il Giovane. The gallery is supported by two square pillars of marble carved in honeysuckle and grotesques. Although Ruskin could not but commend the quality of the carving he condemned the pillars outright for being no more architecture than two wooden posts. The marble images of two children 'under the Organs (the work of the famous Praxitiles)', which Fynes Moryson admired, are no longer to be seen, and it is difficult to believe that his attribution was more than wild hearsay. The balustrade of the gallery is composed of large pierced circular panels of wood, and the ceiling above it of intarsia partly gilded. This gallery was originally used as the nuns' choir of a neighbouring convent of Poor Clares attached to the church by a corridor. And to create the illusion that the nuns are still here (needless to say they were dispersed by Napoleon) the strains of a Bach Brandenburg Concerto are made to issue from a transistor carefully concealed in the gallery. The organ doors of *The Annunciation* painted by Giovanni Bellini expressly for a room leading off the gallery were removed in 1897 and are now in the Accademia. As Hugh Honour remarks, it is 'the one thing missing in this perfect synthesis of early Renaissance art'.

A straight flight of fourteen steps leads to the tribune which is built over the crypt, or sacristy. Behind a marble balustrade wooden stalls are decorated with what James Morris calls 'adorable' figures. 'I cannot imagine the most truculent of atheists failing to remove his hat as he enters this irresistible sanctuary.' At either end of the balustrade a pulpit hangs over the nave, its eagle lectern slightly tilted to accommodate an opened Bible. On the exquisitely carved newels of the balustrade are posted three-quarter length statuettes of the *Virgin Mary*, the *Archangel Gabriel, St Francis* and *St Clare*, definitely by Tullio Lombardo. Mary, with hands clasped across her breast, wears an expression of absolute resignation, acceptance and innocence.

A high archway gives access from tribune to presbytery. It is open to criticism for meeting the arch of the nave vault in a clumsy fashion, and indicates that the presbytery was in fact an afterthought. In the course of building the shrine for the holy icon Angelo Amadi and the other donors decided to enlarge the chapel into a church. The pair of returned pilasters which form the opening are carved from top to bottom by Antonio Lombardo with traditional classical arabesques. On the socle, or base of each are depicted in high relief *putti* standing on the long tails of mermaids which entwine their necks, and holding the mermaids' hands. Very pagan these emblems are too. Ruskin was terribly shocked. While allowing that all the sculpture should be examined with care and attention 'as the best possible examples of a bad style', the subjects appalled him. What he particularly objected to was the treatment of a child's head on the plinth of the right-hand pilaster. 'The men who could carve a child's head so perfectly must have been wanting in all human feeling', he railed, 'to cut it off and tie it by the hair to a vine leaf.' On the contrary the head is not decapitated because there is no body to have decapitated it from. The sculptor carved a bodiless but winged head of an angel, two tresses of whose hair are tied gracefully to a twig of leaves. It is an entirely fanciful conception and the face has a blissfully contented expression.

Within the square presbytery under a dome stands the high altar upon which the four Evangelists framed by roundels in the pendentives look down. They are in bas-relief by the Lombardi. The lace-like pair of perforated panels which form a low screen to the high altar are faultlessly carved with honeysuckles, dolphins and tridents. There is nothing to prevent you closely examining Vittoria's bronzes at either end of the altar. They represent *St Peter* and *St Anthony Abbot*, founder of the earliest monasteries, who for years lived on bread and water partaken once a day, and lived to be 105. These bronzes are not quite the only things of later date than the church itself, belonging as they do to the end of the sixteenth century. Even so they conform to the Lombardic style as does the insipidly derivative reredos of 1887 which frames the miracle-working icon of Francesco Amadi's *Madonna and Child*. One must not judge it too harshly for it commemorates the re-instatement of the church, after years of desolation when it became the haunt of pigeons, to a place of worship once again. This was largely due to the personal intervention and financial help of Queen Margharita of Savoy.

Free and easy is the way in which Santa Maria dei Miracoli is administered. When I was last there a corkless bottle, labelled *Vino moscato per Santa Messa*, a quarter full, was propped against the altar step. I narrowly missed spilling it. And on the altar a silver pyx was left with a cascade of wafers issuing from it. I happened to be on the floor searching for Ruskin's severed head when, on turning, I saw an old priest approaching with his attendant server. I struggled to my feet in order to slip away as decently as possible when with a conciliatory gesture the priest mumbled, '*S'accomodi!*' 'Please do not disturb yourself.' I resisted a natural inclination to disobey him and went on searching. But I really could not do it for long. By the time I reached the lady selling postcards under the gallery she had switched off the Brandenburg Concerto in mid bar. I waved a friendly goodbye to her as she flung the unsold cards into a capacious bag. 'When he gets going,' she said in Italian, nodding towards the altar with disapproval, 'there is no stopping him.' Her implication was that whereas the old priest had no objection to a myopic elderly gentleman crawling round the altar on hands and knees he drew the line at buying and selling in the temple of the Almighty during the celebration of holy mass. 'I may as well go home now,' she added ruefully. 'In any case it's beginning to get dark.'

SAN GIORGIO MAGGIORE

1559 – 1614

> I stood in Venice on the Bridge of Sighs;
> A palace and a prison on each hand:
> I saw from out the waves her structures rise
> As from the stroke of the Enchanter's wand.

Thus on 26 June 1817 Lord Byron opened Canto IV of *Childe Harold's Pilgrimage*. Within less than a month he had finished the first draft of 126 stanzas. He was dwelling upon the thousand years and more in which Venice had risen from the ocean like some magical exhalation. But if the concept really did occur to him on the Bridge of Sighs then the only shuttered view before his eyes down the narrow Rio di Palazzo Ducale was of San Giorgio Maggiore; for nothing else is visible from that particular stance. A rather indifferent portrait was painted during his short Venetian sojourn, of the poet standing in a sort of romantic Vandyke cloak and pose on the Ponte di Paglia with the Bridge of Sighs behind him. His eyes are firmly fixed upon the island on the other side of St Mark's Canal.

Before the year 790 the island of San Giorgio Maggiore was known as the island of cypresses, there being a small wood of these trees among orchards and vineyards. When Doge Agnello Partecipazio founded the Ducal Palace about AD 814 he erected a mill on the island for grinding his own corn. Then in 982 Doge Tribuno Memmo, in compensation for a grave injury done by his family to the Morosini, gave the island to Zuane Morosini who established a Benedictine monastery where formerly a small chapel to St George had stood. For over 700 years the Benedictines remained undisturbed. In 1806 the monastery was suppressed and the island handed over to the Austrian army as a barracks.

The tenth-century monastic church was dedicated to St Stephen when that saint's corpse, having been seized in Constantinople, was transferred to Venice. Doge Ordelaffo Falier assisted with his own strong arms in carrying the coffin which enclosed the protomartyr's precious remains to the high altar in 1109. Thereafter successive doges would, on the Feast of St Stephen, cross over to the island to venerate his bones. For some reason which is not clear the protomartyr Stephen fell, as is the way of saints, into disfavour and the mythical St George was nominated guardian of the island in his stead. The adjective *maggiore*, meaning greater, was appended in order to distinguish it from the Benedictine fathers' lesser island, San Giorgio d'Alega (St George of the Seaweed). Meanwhile the Benedictine community flourished as a seat of study and devotion, in spite of the destruction of church and monastic buildings in a devastating earthquake of 1223. Thomas Coryate, visiting the island in 1611, remarked that St Stephen's bones still lay enclosed under a goodly altar of red marble. He pronounced the place 'passing sumptuous' and 'the fairest and richest monastery without comparison in all Venice . . . Now they are much occupied in building'.

Coryate came on the scene just when major operations were in hand. He would have seen the northern façade of the monks' *dormitorium*, which survives, by Giovanni Buora, an associate of Pietro Lombardo, with its three stone lunette gables over eye windows and round-headed arcades, like a miniature Lombardo palace. The actual roof lines of the *dormitorium* do not correspond with the lunette gables which were built unashamedly for aesthetic effect. Coryate would also have seen the library designed by Michelozzi at the instigation and expense of Cosimo de' Medici the elder, who had been given asylum on the island during his brief exile from Florence in 1434. His absent host was Pope Euganeus IV, himself a Benedictine who had formerly been Abbot Gabriele Condulmaro. Cosimo was so impressed by the monks' rare collection of codices, incunabulae and illuminated manuscripts that in gratitude he decided to provide a worthy setting for them. But three years after the English itinerant's visit this splendid building was destroyed to make room for the great cloister, which had been designed by Palladio.

Coryate would also have seen the Cloister of the Cypresses which Giovanni Buora began and his son Andrea completed in 1593. The present impressive library of massive carved bookshelves he would not have seen, for it was not built until the 1640s; nor the wonderful Baroque staircase of double flight and impressive arcading by Longhena, also dating from the 1640s, which set the pace for the ambitious conventual architects of south Germany and Austria in the ensuing century. These accessories, including Palladio's stark refectory, as befitted a strict religious order, and even starker corridor of the dormitorium (called *la Manica Lunga*, the long sleeve, 420 feet in length) from which the monks' cells are entered, may only be visited by special permission.

As for the refectory, Palladio made it deliberately simple. He merely relieved total bareness by an ingenious groined vault in the centre of the room and persuaded the Benedictines to commission Veronese's sparkling *Marriage Feast at Cana*. This marvellous picture was painted in 1563 for the end wall behind the abbot's seat. After the fall of the Republic it was taken down in sections and looted by Napoleon. It is now in the Louvre. William Beckford was bowled over by it. Yet for a connoisseur of art, his comments were hardly illuminating. He reserved praise for the glowing colours, the multitude of figures and the cunning perspectives meant to accord with and complement the architecture of the room. 'The guests appear a very genteel, decent sort of people', he wrote sardonically, 'well used to the mode of their time and accustomed to miracles.' He also feasted his eyes on the provisions about to be consumed by the Fathers at table. He pretended that the Republic encouraged monks and clerics to appear to the Venetian citizens as men of flesh and blood in order to prevent them being considered super-human and so becoming a danger to the state.

It is the existing church which concerns us. So successful was the refectory deemed to be that in 1565 Palladio was appointed by the Benedictines proto for the rebuilding of the church. The Council of Trent had ended only two years previously, having reaffirmed the basic articles of the Catholic faith, laid tremendous emphasis on the celebration of the sacraments, and decreed how churches should henceforth be planned so as to allow separate spaces for the laity, for a dominant high altar to enshrine the sacred mysteries, and for the devotions of the regular clergy. The Counter Reformation was in full swing, and the Tridentine decrees provided a blistering counterblast to the Reformed Churches of Luther and Calvin.

To some extent Palladio's plan was predetermined by that of the previous church. But apart from being based on a Latin cross, it in no way conformed to the traditional type of Benedictine abbey. The unfortunate thing was that, although designed by Palladio, the façade was begun, altered and finished by another between 1602 and 1610, thirty years after Palladio was dead. The guidebooks claim that this architect was Scamozzi, Palladio's distinguished disciple, who bore the same close relation to his great master as did John Webb to Inigo Jones. Rudolf Wittkower, however, discovered that he was Simone Sorella, a less well known architect who built the leaning tower of San Giorgio dei Greci. San Giorgio Maggiore was not the first of Palladio's church façades designed on the temple theme, but the second. The first was that of San Francesco della Vigna. The third to be designed by the master was that of Il Redentore, raised on steps as was the Pantheon in Roman times, and completed in 1592, before San Giorgio's but, like it, after Palladio's death. There is closer resemblance between San Francesco and Il Redentore than between San Giorgio, as carried out, and either of the other two. In wrestling with the awkward problem of giving a classical temple front to a basilican church with high central nave and low lateral aisles Palladio resolved it by antique precedent.

Goethe was one of the first people of modern times to recognize that Palladio was strongly imbued with the spirit of the ancients. He referred to him as 'this extraordinary man' who seemed to be standing beside him, saying, 'This or that I did against my will. Nevertheless I did it because it was the closest approximation to my ideal possible under the circumstances.' Goethe went on, 'The more I think about him the more strongly I feel that, when he looked at the height and width of an old church or house for which he had to make a new façade, he must have said to himself, "How can you give this building the noblest form possible?"'

Rudolf Wittkower in extremely learned treatises has answered this hypothetical question by tracing the ways in which the early Renaissance architects had tackled the problem. Alberti in Sant'Andrea in Mantua contrived a temple front to look as though it covered both nave and aisles – but not entirely satisfactorily. Bramante at Santa Maria di San Satiro, in Milan, next used parts of pediments to cover the aisles while raising another storey to cover the nave. The two lower storeys of nave and aisles were contained under one unbroken entablature. Peruzzi at Carpi Cathedral used the giant order for the nave and a small order for the aisles. Palladio found none of these essays organic or in accord with the doctrines of antiquity. He evolved from his predecessors' experiments what proved to be the ultimate solution of the Classical temple front applied to a Christian basilica of high nave and low lateral aisles.

What did he do? He went back to the Pantheon in Rome, that is to say by using one pediment to crown the portico and another further back attached to the high attic, the latter necessarily recessed and appearing to the spectator on the ground to be broken by the advanced portico. With San Francesco and Il Redentore both portico columns and aisle pilasters are on the same plinth level. With San Giorgio as carried out this is not the case. The portico half-columns are raised on high plinths, the aisle pilasters are on the ground level and their entablature is carried across the temple front. A further anomaly lies in the little aedicules of the aisles being raised on grotesquely high plinths the same level as those which carry the colossal half-columns of the nave.

These objections may seem frivolous. They are certainly academic but once pointed out cause the viewer a certain unease. The fact is that part of a drawing by Palladio exists to prove that he intended the two architectural orders of the San

Giorgio façade to rise from the same level. There is little doubt that he would have been horrified did he know the hash that Sorella was to make of his harmoniously contrived façade. And harmonious is the word. Palladio inherently believed that harmony, as in music, was the very essence of classical architecture and that it could be arrived at only by the strictest mathematical proportions. He devised proportions of the façades and interiors of his churches and villas according to a unit of measurement termed the *modulus* which he believed the Roman architects had established for posterity.* Hugh Honour has ably summarized the somewhat arcane principles of this man of genius. From the study of a series of musical consonances Palladio 'derived ratios . . . based on the arithmetical and harmonic mean, and the relationship of one part of a building to another and the whole. It is therefore no flower of speech to talk of the harmony of Palladio's churches and villas. They are as mathematically complex and harmoniously satisfying as the fugues of Bach.' His architecture was to be copied or adapted by architects down to the end of the eighteenth century, and even beyond.

No matter how much tampered with by Palladio's successor, the snow-white front of San Giorgio's church in Istrian stone, prominent in the great pink mass of brick buildings and backed

*'The façade of San Francesco della Vigna may be used for a demonstration. In accordance with Vitruvius, a unit of measurement, the *modulus*, was applied to all dimensions in the building. The basic unit is the diameter of the small columns which is 2 feet (*piedi*). The diameter of the large order is 2 moduli. i.e. 4 feet. The height of the small columns is 20 feet (10 moduli), that of the larger ones 40 feet (20 moduli). In both cases the ratio of diameter to height is 1:10 and that of the small order to the large order is 1:2. The width of the intercolumniation of the centre bay is again 20 feet (10 moduli). Without giving more details it is evident that, just as in Alberti's S. Maria Novella, simple ratios of the same modulus are effective throughout the building. But this is not the whole story. *Symmetria* for Palladio meant more than applied arithmetic. The whole centre part in front of the nave is 27 moduli wide. Palladio, inheriting a long tradition, conceived his structures as reflections and echoes of that cosmic order which Pythagoras and Plato had revealed.' From Rudolf Wittkower's *Architectural Principles in the Age of Humanism*, 1949, page 86.

San Giorgio Maggiore

Santa Maria dei Miracoli

Santa Maria della Salute

by green trees has, in Henry James's words, 'a success beyond all reason. It is a success of position, of colour . . . a kind of suffusion of rosiness'. It occupies one of the most spectacular sites in all Venice, the compelling eye-catcher from the Piazzetta and the Riva degli Schiavoni, set at a most suitable distance and angle. Everything about the grouping and its perspective – the porticoed temple, the flanking walls with ball crests, the great dome, the pair of towers with onion cupolas in the rear, punctuated by the attenuated campanile – is from the picturesque point of view serene and right.

William Beckford was gloriously unaffected by Scamozzi's or Sorella's architectural solecisms. On 3 August 1780 he landed on the island as dawn broke. He called the church

> by far the most perfect and beautiful edifice my eyes ever beheld. When my first transport was a little subsided, and I had examined the graceful design of each particular ornament and united the just proportion and grand effect of the whole in my mind, I planted my umbrella on the margin of the sea [the harbour was not constructed until the 1820s], and reclining under its shade, my feet dangling over the waters, viewed the vast range of palaces opposite. [Whereupon] I ate my grapes, and read Metastasio, undisturbed by offiousness or curiosity. When the sun became too powerful, I entered the nave, and applauded the genius of Palladio.

Beckford was at the date twenty years old, still the owner of Fonthill Splendens, that great and grand Palladian house in Wiltshire. His tastes were to change, as they continuously changed in advance of his contemporaries', and by 1800 he had pulled down classical Splendens to raise within his park the Gothic fantasy, Fonthill Abbey.

Before the middle of the nineteenth century, when the Gothic Revival was predominant, Ruskin was writing that it was 'impossible to conceive a design more gross, more barbarous, more childish in conception, more servile in plagiarism, more insipid in result, more contemptible under every point of rational regard' than the façade of San Giorgio. And his opinion came to be shared by his contemporaries and successors.

For Henry James, in spite of his encomiums of the monastic buildings as a group, denounced San Giorgio as 'an ugly Palladian church', almost, one feels, because Ruskin would have expected him to do so. To his credit the Ruskins' great friend Rawdon Brown, who lived in Venice, rebuked them in no uncertain terms, in a letter to Effie dated 12 January 1850, for their dismissive attitude to Palladio. He said that he was profoundly moved by the rays of the evening sun falling on the front of San Giorgio, 'whereas you would most fastidiously frown on them, because Palladio (who, believe me, must have devoted a good three months at least to the study of architecture) eschewed the pointed arch: you lose much enjoyment by this disdainful humour, to say nothing of injustice to the dead . . . I consider myself not less indebted here to Sansovino and to Baldassar Longhena than to the unknown architect of the Ducal Palace.' To this reproachful letter from a permanent resident of long standing in Venice the Ruskins, who after all were only occasional visitors, gave no answer.

Before you enter the church you will notice with satisfaction that between the pairs of great columns, and within niches, stand full-length statues of *St Stephen* and *St George*, appropriately sharing the honour of dedication. They are carved and signed by Giulio del Moro, about whom nobody seems to know anything. The pair of aedicules of the wings on their preposterously high plinths enshrine sarcophagi with busts by the same sculptor of the no less appropriate Doges Tribuno Memmo (who gave the island to Zuane Morosini) and Sebastiano Ziani (who brought about the reconciliation of Pope Alexander III and Frederick Barbarossa). Rather oddly, these doges are made to wear the dogal cap the wrong way round, the *còrnu* in the front instead of at the back, in the way in which a dead cavalry officer's boots are turned in the stirrup to face the horse's withers in his funeral procession.

There is nothing quite like the interior of San Giorgio in the whole of Catholic Europe. On entry you are struck by the luminosity, totally unlike the twilight of medieval basilicas and even Renaissance fanes. It is like being inside an ancient

Roman temple that has been given a roof. The grey stone columns, arches and entablatures do nothing to darken the glistening white background walls. The coldly mathematical, almost Grecian precision of the architecture is relieved from all flatness by as many as 44 niches filled with feigned instead of the marble statues intended, but never executed. The painted chiaroscuro serves its purpose well. So too the red and orange squares, laid diagonally, of the pavement, the rich components of the high altar behind a balustrade and the marvellous paintings of the communicating side altars (when these are not taken out of their frames for restoration) provide welcome colour and warmth. Nave, aisles and transept with terminal apses are separated by chunky piers. On both sides of the nave giant half-columns on high plinths soar past the coupled pilasters and pulvinated entablatures which carry the arches. The half-columns in their turn boldly carry a running entablature which supports the clerestory. The nave has a barrel vault and the aisles have quadripartite roofs. The entablature of the half-columns is like a thick tight belt holding the two stages of the interior together. Viewed from the foot of any one plinth the entablature looks almost grotesque, forming zig-zags and sharp breaks. Viewed from the west entrance door the vaulting presents a recession of semi-circles from nave to presbytery and away into the distant choir. Over the crossing is a timely diversion in the sweep of the balustrade under the cupola, an ellipse, as it were, in reverse.

The west doorway through which you entered is flanked by blue-grey engaged columns on plinths the same height as those of the giant nave columns. On the west wall a painting by Paolo Piazza represents *The Signoria supplicating Our Lady* to bring to an end the plague of 1619. And a stone records the vow made by Doge Alvise Mocenigo I in September 1576 to have the present church reconstructed when the terrible pestilence raging in that year should end. Within niches stucco statues of *The Four Evangelists* are signed by Vittoria and dated 1574.

In the second chapel of the right aisle is a survivor of the old church – a *Crucifixion* in wood. Attributed to Brunelleschi (and disputed by Lorenzetti) it is a very ghastly thing, although a work of distinction. Blood oozes from the cheek and chest of Christ. The head is drooping, the mouth is open and the hair is matted and clotted with sweat. In the third chapel the brother saints *Cosmas and Damian*, patrons of surgeons and physicians, were painted *circa* 1592. If the 'tumultuous conception of the whole' can be attributed to Tintoretto, Lorenzetti pontificates, the operation of the painting is by collaborators. He makes the same pronunciation about *The Coronation of the Virgin* in the right arm of the transept. On either side of this painting a pair of three-legged bronze candelabra are thirteenth-century Romanesque, a rare survival. The feet are formed of three angels embracing.

Each arm of the transept has an aedicule on the curve, supported by wavy grey coupled columns of marble, with concave pediments. The rich and splendid altar on the right of the presbytery displays several novel features. *The Madonna and Saints* by Sebastiano Ricci conveys a Rococo verve and a boldness of contrasting colours in the bright blue dress of the Madonna seated to the left of the picture and carrying a palm, and the scarlet robe of an accompanying saint who leans on a plinth the better to read a book. This painting, which anticipates Tiepolo, is dated 1708.

Both Sebastiano and his nephew Marco Ricci were in England at the beginning of the eighteenth century under the patronage of the Duke of Manchester, who was the English Ambassador to Venice. Marco, the first to go, took with him in 1708 Sebastiano's pupil Pellegrini who did a good deal of work at Kimbolton Castle, the duke's seat in Huntingdonshire, and Castle Howard in Yorkshire. Sebastiano was persuaded by his nephew to join them in 1711 by the prospect of painting the dome of St Paul's. The scheme came to nothing. Instead he left in our country a masterpiece in a fresco of *The Resurrection* in the half-dome of Chelsea Hospital Chapel. Two of his large mythology canvases still hang on the staircase of Burlington House, Piccadilly. The Italians' stay in England, in spite of the encouragement by the circle of Lords Burlington and Kent of all things Italian, was cut short by the hostile and chauvinistic rivalry of Thornhill and his artist compatriots.

The presbytery and monks' choir in San Giorgio were both begun after Palladio's death, but are part and parcel of the great architect's conception. Each is approached by a short flight of steps as though to emphasize by the difference of levels the separate significance of the units. Theatrical and breathtaking though the presbytery is with its view through a screen of fluted Corinthian columns under the organ, there is something a trifle tight and congested about the aedicule and flanking openings which accommodate the organ pipes. The concave arcade of the Redentore presbytery makes a more scenographic screen between it and the choir. On the other hand the array of giant columns and pilasters at the sides of the sanctuary of San Giorgio when seen from the nave are like a row of trees planted in perspective in order to lead the eye to some focal object beyond. Capitals and entablatures are juxtaposed as the wings depicting a forest glade on a stage would be. Purists will find the arrangement faulty and puritans shockingly dramatic.

Just within the balustrade separating nave from sanctuary are a pair of showy bronze candelabra by Nicolò Roccatagliata (1598), one of the great workers in that metal of the *cinquecento*. The build-up of each candelabrum is like a feat of the *Forze d'Ercole*, of which gymnastic performances the Venetians were so fond, in that three *putti* hold a central urn, which in turn holds three more *putti* who carry a superstructure on which three dolphins support the candle-holder with their tails – an ingenious and delicious acrobatic.

Facing each other on either side of the sanctuary are two of Tintoretto's greatest achievements of his old age, painted in 1594 when he was nearly eighty. That on the right is *The Last Supper*, a scene almost supernaturally portrayed. From a flaming lamp-bowl suspended over the table, which is set diagonally on a pavement laid diagonally, light is diffused upon the spread cloth, the plates of fruit and glass vessels, and the maidservant reaching from a basket into which a dog impertinently nuzzles for a standing dish which she passes to a servitor. The young Christ administering the sacrament to his neighbouring disciple and the disciples themselves are thrown into shadow by the dazzling fire from their haloes. Above the company evanescent angels sweep and swoop like swallows under the crepuscular ceiling. The movement, the solemnity and the mystery combined are without parallel in Renaissance painting. The setting for *The Gathering of Manna* is very different. It takes place in an open landscape. All is peaceful and arcadian. Rustic figures like harvesters are gathering manna as it might be the fruits of the earth amidst fresh verdure, trickling waters, hills and flowers. The subject was intended to be a reminder of the supreme importance of the eucharist, recently stressed by the Council of Trent.

Raised on steps the high altar stands before the central intercolumn of the screen. The arrangement is an innovation in that there is no reredos to block the view through the screen into the choir. A bronze group of *The Four Evangelists* desperately upholds the world on the top of which stands the Eternal Father in benediction. On the globe's face the Holy Ghost is depicted hovering over the crucified Christ. This group is the work of Gerolamo Campagna (1591–3), who also carved the beautiful *Madonna and Child* surrounded by *putti* in glistening Carrara marble in the left aisle. On either side of the high altar stands a bronze angel of the mid-seventeenth century.

Beyond the columned screen of the sanctuary is reached the long rectangular choir with apsed end. The room, though fine in itself, seems unrelated to the church, but it contains 48 wooden stalls inlaid with episodes from the life of St Benedict, worked between 1594 and 1598. On the arms of each stall a *putto* rides a dolphin; yet no one *putto* is like another. The artist was a Fleming, Albrecht van der Brulle from Antwerp, aided by a Venetian, Gaspare Gatti. On the newels of the balustrade which forms a passage between screen and choir are two elegant bronzes by Roccatagliata of *St George* and *St Stephen*. Théophile Gautier observed that the head of the first was more like that of Lord Byron than any representation of the poet he knew. He saw in its tilt the disdain of the British aristocrat and in the contracted lip the satiric sneer of Don Juan. How flattered, he thought, would Byron have been had he ever noticed it. In fact the little *St George* bears hardly any resemblance to what we know of Byron's likeness from innumerable paintings and busts. Only in the shape of the head and the curls of the hair is there a remote resemblance. On the contrary, the hooded eyes and weak chin recall photographs of the famous Edwardian hostess Lady Desborough.

If we take a narrow staircase leading from the right-hand side of the aforementioned passage we climb to the Cappella Superiore, or Sala Capitolare. It was here that the Cardinal-Camerlengo summoned all the cardinals who could reach Venice to attend a conclave for the election of a new pope in 1799. The late Pius VI, a saintly man, had been driven out of Rome from pillar to post, treated with the utmost ferocity by French troops, and had died at Valence in August. Napoleon vowed that never again was there to be a papal election. But the Camerlengo, a man in his mid-seventies, was determined that an election would take place, if not in Rome, then no matter where. This dignitary happened to be the Cardinal of York, in other words the *de jure* King Henry IX of Great Britain, only surviving legitimate grandson of James II. For three and a half months the assembled cardinals remained incarcerated in the Benedictine monastery on the island of San Giorgio Maggiore. During the weary confabulations which accompanied this papal election, the Cardinal of York who, formerly rich, had been reduced to near penury by the Curia's expulsion by the French from Rome and the confiscation of his property and possessions, was cheered by the news that King George III of England (to him the Elector of Hanover) had graciously granted him a small pension. It was enough to keep the wolf from the door.

On 14 March 1800 Barnabò Chiaramonte, Bishop of Imola, was elected and took the name of Pius VII. From the Sala Capitolare a small door opens upon the chimney whence the emission of a final puff of white smoke announced to the perplexed citizens of Venice that a new pontiff was elected. A plaque indicates the stall (easily found) in which the Cardinal-King sat daily throughout the harshest months of an intolerably cold Venetian winter. Over the altar hangs *St George slaying the Dragon*, a studio version in tempera, dated 1516 and signed Vittorio Carpaccio, of the better known painting by the artist in the Scuola di San Giorgio degli Schiavoni. Included on the *predella* are four panels of further episodes of St George, brought from the Abbey of Santa Maria del Pero at Monastier.

Before leaving San Giorgio you are well advised to mount the campanile, that conspicuous punctuation of the great monastic congeries of buildings. It is attached to the north-east angle of the church. Like that of St Mark's, the original tower collapsed in 1773, killing a monk and causing, as one of his brethren remarked, 'a dismal vacancy among the marvels' of the island. In 1791 it was rebuilt by a Brother of the Order from Bologna more or less on the lines of St Mark's tower, and certainly with the utmost architectural propriety. Crowning the rosy brick shaft and the belfry of white Istrian stone, the candle-snuffer spire flaunts a golden St George who rotates with the winds.

Formerly the visitor was obliged to climb a wooden ramp with shallow steps, manageable by a mule, but now the alternative method takes even longer. You are obliged to wait, listening to the chatter of the other tourists drown the piped strains of *Così fan Tutte* (an odd choice of opera), for what seems an eternity. Finally, for a few *lire*, a charming young priest allows a small group at a time to enter the lift. You soar upwards. From the balustraded terrace wonderful views, better than those from St Mark's campanile, are obtained over the city to the islands of the lagoons and into the open Adriatic. The best time to choose is the evening before the sun sets behind the Euganean hills.

The superb condition of the monastic buildings and church of San Giorgio Maggiore is due to the Giorgio Cini Foundation. In 1951 Count Vittorio Cini acquired the whole island, then still occupied by the military. He restored the buildings from one end to the other and instituted the flourishing Centro di Cultura e Civiltà in memory of his son, a heroic figure of the last war, Count Giorgio Cini, who was killed in a flying accident. Where formerly Benedictine monks led an active life devoted to the Christian faith and learning, now accredited lay students from all over the world congregate in diligence and tranquillity for research after the arts and sciences.

SANTA MARIA DELLA SALUTE

1631–81

If San Giorgio Maggiore has the finest site *off* Venice, then the Madonna della Salute has the finest site *in* Venice, for it occupies that spit or triangle of the Dorsoduro which commands the entrance of ships and boats to the Giudecca Canal and the Grand Canal. Could any other site be more glorious or more commanding? The Punta della Salute is as sharp as the point of a needle. In the past it served as the connecting link, at moments of threatened invasion, of two enormous iron chains, extending to the moles of St Mark's and San Giorgio. As near the *punta* as can be stands the enchanting little Dogana whence watch could be kept of all goods, contraband or licit, entering the city from the sea. Henry James saw it in a romantic light:

> The charming architectural promontory of the Dogana stretches out the most graceful of arms, balancing in its hand the gilded globe on which revolves the delightful satirical figure of a little weather-cock of a woman. This Fortune, this Navigation, or what ever she is called – she surely needs no name – catches the wind in the bit of drapery of which she has divested her rotary bronze loveliness.

The Dogana, a version of the Tower of the Winds in Athens, square with three porticoes, acts as a sort of fo'c'sle attached to the splayed custom house, as it were the bows of a great ship of state, of which the domes and towers of the Salute arise like clustered funnels and masts amidships. The last monument is so proud and prominent, so massively conspicuous, that comparatively few critics have dared seriously to attack it. Even Ruskin found it impressive on account of its position, size and general proportions, despite lambasting the grotesque Renaissance of which it was a product. He admitted that its architect had a natural gift of massing and grouping his units. Besides, Turner had admired it from a distance and one needed not to approach it too closely. James Fergusson in his monumental *A History of Architecture* published in the 1860s was constrained reluctantly to agree:

> Considering the age in which it was erected, it is singularly pure, and it is well adapted to its site . . . Externally it is open to the criticism of being rather too overloaded with decoration; But there is very little even of this that is unmeaning, or put there merely for the sake of ornament.

And Horatio Brown, writing towards the end of the nineteenth century, acknowledged that, though wilful, it was a picturesque object. Picturesque is just what the great Venetian Baroque painters found it. Canaletto for instance could never leave it alone. He introduced it into nearly every view of the city he painted. And it would be tedious to enumerate those of his distinguished successors, Venetian and foreign, who have likewise immortalized it on canvas.

It is almost incredible that we can today see this great church – and indeed nearly all Venetian monuments – exactly as Turner, Guardi and even Canaletto saw them. Here, with the exception of the wall built in 1818 to connect the steps of the church to the seminary on its left and crowned with statues of the seventeenth and eighteenth centuries, everything is unchanged. The seminary, a plain structure with horizontal string courses, serves as an admirable foil, whereas on the right the polygonal apse of the one-time abbey of San Gregorio, with vertical windows and plum brick buttresses, provides the happiest illustration of sharawadgi, that artful incongruity in the style of a background object which enhances the majesty of the predominant feature of a composition.

We seem to be approaching Santa Maria della Salute from the Grand Canal which is the fittest way. The *traghetto* from Harry's Bar takes us across. We thus experience how Henry James and Robert Browning and Mrs Bronson's other

distinguished protégés saw it from the windows of her palace, the Casa Alvise (now the Hotel Regina), so directly opposite the Salute that from the balcony 'your eye, crossing the Canal, seems to find the key-hole [except that there is no key-hole] of the great door right in a line with it', according to the novelist.

> She is more ample and serene, more seated at her door, than all the copyists have told us, with her domes and scrolls, her scolloped buttresses and statues forming a pompous crown, and her wide steps disposed on the ground like the train of a robe [a good simile, this]. This fine air of the woman of the world is carried out by the well-bred assurance with which she looks in the direction of her old-fashioned Byzantine neighbour [a not so accurate allusion to the Gothic San Gregorio].

Mrs Bronson was one of those sweet, generous and infinitely hospitable American widows who in the most innocent and disarming manner wished to make happy her men friends, especially when they were eminent. She allowed Browning, and his sister, to rent at a preposterously low figure the Palazzo Giustiniani-Recanti, which was tacked on to the back of the Alvise. Robert was naive enough to admire the Salute unreservedly. 'Is it possible', he wrote simply, 'that wise men disapprove of those quaint buttresses? To me they rise out of the sea like gigantic shells.' But then he made no claim to understand architecture. He loved watching from the windows of the Ca' Alvise the sea gulls dipping into the Canal water. He admired them more than the pigeons.

The steps do indeed sweep in generous folds before the three central façades of the octagon down to an ample pavement, before spreading into the Grand Canal the very fringe of the robe's train, stained by green seaweed. There is a memorial inscription carved on a marble flag of the top step to one Marcus Trevisano, who renovated the church in 1909. The pavement before the church and the *campo* in front of the patriarchal seminary is one continuous tesselated carpet in a uniform pattern of rectangles, ovals and circles.

Young William Beckford was lost in admiration of the majestic and inerrable scene as his gondola drew up at the slippery steps below the entrance. He made the Salute his first visit before dawn on an early August morning. He had come from the Hotel Leon Bianco, just beyond the Rialto Bridge where he had arrived the previous evening.

> To criticize columns or pediments of the different façades [he wrote wisely] would be time lost; since one glance upon the worst view that has been taken of them, conveys a far better idea than the most elaborate description. The great bronze portal opened whilst I was standing on the steps which lead to it, and discovered the interior of the dome, where I expatiated in solitude; no mortal appearing except an old priest who trimmed the lamps, and muttered a prayer before the high altar, still wrapped in shadows. The sunbeams began to strike against the windows of the cupola just as I left the church, and was wafted across the waves to the spacious platform of S. Giorgio Maggiore . . .

But before you enter the great octagon the history of this extreme limb of the Dorsoduro and the reasons for the existence of the Salute must be considered.

Anyone landing from a boat on the triangular promontory at the beginning of the thirteenth century would find himself in a boggy, marshy territory, uncultivated and neglected. It was part of the property of the monks of San Gregorio, whose abbey was established on the west side of the *rio* of their name. In 1256 Doge Raniero Zen cleared the ground and erected on the promontory a monastery and church, which he dedicated to the Holy Trinity, for the benefit of the German Knights who had helped Venice defeat the Genoese that year. The White Brothers of the Trinity, as the knights became known, made the monastery the first house of their Order and added buildings. Shops arose and a *squero*, or yard for the building of boats, to carry the salt which they traded in. The White Brothers also built a church, Santa Maria dell'Umiltà, at the south end of the Rio di San Gregorio for the benefit of the inhabitants of the Giudecca on their first reaching the Dorsoduro.

In 1550 the White Brothers were obliged to cede to Ignatius Loyola, the formidable first General of the Society of Jesus, the church of the Umiltà and towards the end of the century their land adjoining the salt factory for a house of education. But the Jesuits' sojourn was of short duration. In 1606, during a bitter row between the Republic and the Papacy, Paolo Sarpi advised the doge to expel from Venice the Jesuits, who had supported the pope's solemn but ineffectual interdict against the city. Their place was accordingly taken by the Benedictine monks of San Servolo.

In 1630 Venice was stricken by the most disastrous plague in her long history. The great Italian novelist Manzoni gives a description of it in his famous historical novel *I Promessi Sposi*. A member of the suite of the Mantuan Ambassador to Venice was found to be infected. While the man was in quarantine on the island of San Clemente a carpenter from Venice, happening to work there, caught the infection and brought it back to the city. At once it spread like wildfire, and 46,490 people perished. On 22 October the Senate voted to build a thanks-offering to the Virgin Mary as soon as it ceased. The site of the Trinitarians' seminary, which was moved to Murano, was chosen as the most spectacular available. By November 1631 the plague suddenly abated. On every successive 21 November a thanks-giving service has been held in the present church.

At first a temporary wooden temple was run up on the site donated by the White Brothers of the Trinity. Thither in November 1631 the Doge, the Council of Ten, the Senate, the nobles and the stricken people of Venice assembled.

> The procession started from the high altar of St. Mark's. When it reached the middle of the Piazza a halt was made, while the officers of public health declared that the plague was at an end through the intercession of the Virgin. The announcement was received with salvoes of artillery, the blare of trumpets, and the clang of bells. Then the train moved forward through the narrow streets and crossed the Grand Canal to the wooden church by a bridge of boats. The letter of a contemporary tells us that the day was cloudlessly fine; and this long procession filing across the bridge, the priests in coloured robes, the silver and gold candlesticks, the flags of the various companies, the young nobles in their tight hose and slashed doublets, the elders each with a long white taper in his hand, must have made a picture

that Gentile Bellini should have lived to paint. The Senate did
not neglect their vow, and after a public competition Longhena,
a Venetian, was chosen to build the votive church . . .

Thus wrote Horatio Brown in *Life on the Lagoons*. A picture of
such a bridge of boats by Giuseppe Heintz in the Civico Museo
Correr depicts a bridge formed of boats, not closely packed, but
bearing a gangway of boards on which ships' masts are set
bearing flags and pennons and palm branches. A handrail is
even attached to the masts.

Baldassare Longhena was chosen as architect. He was a
Venetian of thirty-two who had begun life as a sculptor, and
perhaps for the reason that he had hitherto built nothing at all,
his appointment met with a certain amount of criticism. Not
that thirty-two was considered young in the seventeenth
century. The terms of the commission were so onerous that they
did not attract more than eleven applicants for the job. They
stipulated that the monument should be colossal and the cost of
building it cheap; that inside the church the light should be
evenly distributed; that the high altar should be made the focal
point on entry – even before entry – to the extent of dominating
every other aspect of the interior; and that the ambulatory and
side altars should take a subordinate place in the plan. So it is
that when the extremely high entrance doors are opened the
worshipper has a view of receding arches positively guiding
him to the high altar. Only when the centre of the nave is
reached can a roving eye perceive a series of dramatic vistas
through the arches of the ambulatory to the side chapels.
Finally, the last term of the commission was that the whole
affair should create a '*bella figura*', or grand impression, a
condition it pre-eminently fulfilled.

Longhena had been a pupil of Vincenzo Scamozzi and was
therefore inculcated in the Palladian cult. In the competition he
claimed that his circular nave within an octagon was original
and met the demands of the commissioners in that it was meant
to represent the form of a crown in honour of the Madonna. The
claim was not appreciated by his jealous contemporaries until
the church was finished, after the architect had died. Hugh
Honour describes Longhena as 'a short, dapper man, always

dressed in black, of quiet and gentle manners. He had the embarrassing habit of asking everyone he met his opinion of whatever work he then had in hand.' This did not inspire confidence and strikes us as a contradictory trait in the creator of so bold and idiosyncratic a monument. Longhena was none the less quick to take umbrage and seldom relished the advice he sought.

Little time was lost in clearing the ground. The sixteenth-century seminary of the Trinity was razed. 110,772 piles were driven by heavy mallets into the soggy ground to carry the monster in contemplation. By April 1631 the first stone was laid. Not until 9 November 1633 was the fabric seen to rise above the level of the foundations. Twenty years later the church was almost complete and the vast grey dome looked like a bubble about to burst against the azure sky. It is said that the citizens of Venice were amazed, if not flabbergasted, to witness the sudden, overwhelming, almost violent eruption, as from a volcano, on the marshy orchard to which they had been accustomed. The seminary of Umiltà disappeared as it were overnight, engulfed by the monster. The church of Umiltà, becoming more and more neglected and dilapidated, clung on until 1824.

In 1656 the Clerks Regular of Somaschi, an offshoot of the Benedictine Order devoted to the education of poor children, were invited by the Senate to conduct masses in the new temple, and the Republic ordained that paintings and furnishings should be brought from elsewhere to embellish it. In 1670 the Somaschi were given full custody of the church and authorized to build a large college. This was duly undertaken by Longhena, who provided a monumental staircase with ceiling canvas, painted by Antonio Zanchi, of the apotheosis of San Girolamo Emiliani, founder of the Somaschi Order.

Longhena had promised to contrive the Salute church according to the Republic's directions in a way that would pay lasting honour to the Blessed Virgin Mary for having so graciously arrested the plague. He could justly claim that his octagonal plan with chapel projections illustrated the eight-rayed Marian star, or Crown of the Rosary; and that the eye window in the pediment of each projection echoed it. But these Marian touches were in truth subordinate to the classical precedents on which he drew. The octagonal plan of the nave really had a precedent in San Vitale at Ravenna and in no less measure to Palladian themes which Longhena had imbibed from his master, Scamozzi. Original though the projecting chapels are, and wonderfully successful in acting as abutments to sustain the great mass of the drum and dome, their façades derive from Palladio's Zitelle church façade on the Giudecca, with its Roman lunette window in the upper stage. Unlike the Zitelle façade, however, the lower stage of Longhena's chapels is blind; yet even so the niches are a sort of derivation of the shadowed and elongated windows of the Zitelle.

The entrance façade and the two flanking chapel fronts, that is to say the three principal fronts of the eight, are extraordinarily rich. To begin with they are composed of Istrian stone, while the remainder of the exterior is of brick. They are richer than the corresponding west end wall and chapels of the interior, the grandeur of which relies on severely academic lines and masses, adventitious decoration being reduced to a minimum. The exterior entrance façade is a complex example of the triumphal arch type, with four giant Corinthian columns on high plinths. The design is majestic, although made to look somewhat narrow by the very lofty arched doorway and the cramped and crowded niches within the flanking intercolumn spaces. For instance, two over-sized sibyls recline most uncomfortably on the spandrels of the central arch; and on the flanking projections the one large and two smaller statues between the pilasters seem jostling for room.

Statues veritably abound (a total of 130) on the outside of the Salute; statues by Baroque masters such as Francesco Cavrioli, Josse de Corte, Ungaro and Ruer; statues in niches, on pediments, on parapets, on scrolls, on walls, as well as in spandrels. The combination of architecture and sculpture here is a momentous instance of Baroque wholeness. There are reliefs over the segmental Roman windows of the side façades, and masks of winged *putti* on the entablatures. The subjects of

Ca'Rezzonico

Ca'Rezzonico:
Browning's apartment

I Gesuiti – nave and baldachino

I Gesuiti – the pulpit

the statuary visible from the *campo* are in nice contrast to the dreary prophets and fathers of the church, in that they are mostly women with flowing draperies. On the apex of each pediment stands a particularly jolly female. A seductive Eve (actually a copy of the original which fell in a thunderstorm in 1966), her long hair decorously festooned across her stomach, *'dans le déshabille le plus galant, nous souriait du haut d'une corniche sous un rayon de soleil'*, as Gautier was quick to observe on the apex of the left chapel projection. This great forest of statues not only delights the eye but seemingly acts like a series of giant pins locking the heavy structure, so perilously close to the water, firmly to the ground. It induces a sense of security.

The great drum and dome, so out of scale with any other building in Venice and yet so imperious an introduction to the Grand Canal, arise as though pushed skywards by the vast serrated volutes in couples, the most distinctive features of the Salute. Their action is ostensibly that of buttresses, just as they are buttressed by the projecting chapels and frontispieces, on the ends of which they precisely sit. On each scroll incongruously stands the statue of a prophet. Between these extraordinary involutions, known to the Venetians as *gli orecchioni*, the little ears, a pair of long windows, black against the glaring white Istrian stone, are sunk below the balustrade of the drum. Ruskin considered the principal fault of the drum to be the meagreness of these apertures. The wall behind the balustrade terrace forms a circular belt of brick girding the base of the grey hemispherical dome. On the dome, and borne by the close vertical ribs, rests the lantern, surrounded by a circle of obelisks and balls, innovations of Scamozzi and not unwelcome here after the plethora of statues. Crowning the whole the haloed statue of *Our Lady of Salvation*.

Behind the great hemispherical dome of the nave, modelled on St Peter's, Rome, rises the lesser dome of the presbytery with its stilted outline in the Byzantine-Venetian manner of St Mark's. It is flanked by the saucer-like lead roofs of the apses. Behind the presbytery dome and attached to each apse are the twin bell towers with their little cupolas. These towers derive from those of the Zitelle, which however are not free-standing.

The serried rank of domes – the two big white protuberances appearing to Gautier as '*arrondies comme des seins de lait*' – and cupolas are seen to best advantage from the Giudecca. This was recognized by that egregious aesthete Sir William Eden, who conceded that the Salute, otherwise 'decadent and rococo', was beautiful from across the water. In fact the Salute has gathered and reproduced the motifs of all the domes and campanili of Venice. Because of its site on a thin spit of land between wide waters this church is among the few in Venice with two ends absolutely uninterrupted by neighbouring buildings.

The nineteenth century frankly turned its back on the interior architecture of the Salute, concentrating solely on the pictures to be found there. Henry James proclaimed that there was nothing particular to enjoy in the cold and conventional temple save the great Tintorettos. And Henri de Régnier merely remarked on a notice within the door which took his fancy: '*En l'honneur de Dieu et de la Sainte Marie, on est prié de ne pas cracher par terre et de se servir, de préférence, de son mouchoir*', which, bearing in mind why the church was built in the first place, was sound advice while plagues were still a menace. Even he cannot have been unobservant of the dazzling luminosity of the interior, particularly the central nave, a condition which had been laid down by Longhena's commissioners. The light, filtered in abundance through those drum windows which Ruskin found so black and meagre on the outside, is uniformly spread even in the ambulatory, where the density is certainly less.

The enormous central octagon is separated from the ambulatory by eight wedge-shaped piers which carry the massive superstructure. Against the inner side of each quadrilateral pier, which is on the curve, a giant Corinthian column detached and set on a deep plinth (as in Palladio's San Giorgio) carries a balustraded walk at the foot of the drum. This balustrade is broken forward where a projecting socle carries the statue of a prophet. On the two narrowing sides of the pier, coupled pilasters bear the eight arches leading to the ambulatory. On the fourth and necessarily longest side of the pier, coupled three-quarter columns take the ambulatory vault.

Between these three-quarter columns the space is ingeniously filled with a zig-zag of four broken pilasters. Columns, pilasters, and all structural parts are of grey stone against a white-washed background in the manner Palladio copied from the Florentine *quattrocento* churches. The same monochrome treatment applies to drum and dome.

Each section of the octagonal drum is marked by conjoined pairs of Doric pilasters, some broken at the angles and some jammed against the windows in the centre. The latter, poised as they are over the keystones of the ambulatory arches, induce a slightly uneasy feeling. The drum pilasters carry yet another balustrade at the base of the dome; and from them spring the ribs of the dome up to the oculus of the lantern. All these features are of a beige, not grey, stone and the contrast must have been as deliberate as it is satisfactory. Here Longhena struck a chromatic note which Palladio had not sounded. Between the ribs simple white panels get narrower as they reach the top. From the centre of the lantern is hung on a long chain a massive Empire-style candelabrum bearing oil lamps. It was presented to the church by the commune in 1836.

The inside of the nave is kept entirely free of pews and excrescences. Before the entrance to the rotunda a pair of holy water stoups (*acquasantieri*) bear in each basin St Mark and the Baptist (*c.* 1680) in bronze. They merit close scrutiny, for they are minutely chiselled and full of feeling. The pavement is a magnificent concentric circle of marble inlay like a richly patterned carpet of many colours. At the hub a tiny disc bears an inscription on metal, '*Unde origo, inde salus*', and the date, 1631, surrounded by five exquisite stalks of red roses. The ambulatory pavement in squares of Verona marble is bordered by a black and white chequer pattern from pier to pier.

Six chapels open off the ambulatory. The three on the right contain as many paintings by the Neapolitan Luca Giordano, recounting the mysteries of the Virgin. Commissioned in 1685, these paintings are an early prelude to the Rococo style which was to displace the gloomy religious works of seventeenth-century Venetian artists. The three chapels on the left of the ambulatory contain paintings in poor condition. *The Descent of the Holy Spirit*, a late work of Titian brought here from the island of Santo Spirito in 1656 is, notwithstanding, magnificent. A shower of golden light rays from the holy dove hovering with outstretched wings in a Roman lunette window ignites agitated tongues of flame from the heads of the Apostles and the three Marys below. The arms of St Peter and St Mark in the foreground, stretched towards the terrifying vision, complete a triangle of self-deprecating and emotional people. Beneath the altarpiece a marble sarcophagus with a gilt bronze front is ostensibly upheld by two nonchalant angels at the sides, while a group of tiny *putti* are doing all the work underneath. The mahogany confessionals, made to fit the angles between each chapel, are handsome pieces of joinery that should not be overlooked.

The presbytery is approached through an opening immediately opposite the main door. The conception of presbytery and choir beyond, meant to be seen in distant perspective before the church is even entered, follows the Palladian theme. The presbytery is a transverse oblong under the lesser dome (of which the drum has windows and a balustraded walk) and two apses with semi-domes. Each apse contains two ranges of six windows in all. A noteworthy reversal of Longhena's decorative treatment of the nave lies in the whitewashed pilasters against grey walls.

A through view into the choir is partly, and deliberately, obscured so as to heighten the mystery by Longhena's sumptuous high altar. It stands beneath a triumphal arch upheld by four monoliths of Greek marble brought from the Roman amphitheatre at Pola. The elliptical arch springs from an entablature very discoloured and black. The altar of Carrara marble is a pyramid of statuary enshrining a panel of the Madonna and Child, known as *The Holy Virgin of Health*, or *Mesopanditissa*. Brought to Venice as a trophy after the peace treaty with the Turks at the end of the Candian War, it was placed here in 1670. The twelfth-century painting, much restored, and attributed to St Luke, is of less interest than the frame that does honour to it. Josse de Corte, the sculptor who carried out Longhena's design, was a native of Ypres and came to Venice in 1657, remaining in the city until his death there in 1679. Although never his pupil de Corte was a passionate admirer and imitator of Bernini. Forming the apex of the marble pyramid Our Lady holds the Child, both wearing preposterously outsize gold crowns. Below them the figure of Venice kneels to implore a halt to the plague. Opposite her the Plague, impersonated by an old hag, is already taking flight, her arms raised in an attitude of defeat while an angel thrusts a burning torch into her waist. Below Venice and the Plague, and completing the base of the pyramid, the figures of St Mark and St Lawrence Justinian, a medieval Venetian who courted hunger, thirst, lack of sleep, extreme cold and heat and everything disagreeable that might bring him nearer to God, look disturbed by the vision. Angelic caryatids and reliefs of music-playing *putti* complete the collection of Baroque figures remarkable for the vitality of their movements and the swirls and folds of their draperies. To the left of the altar a bronze pascal candlestand by Andrea Bresciano, dated 1570, is composed of a multitude of figures.

It was before the high altar that Horatio Brown one late November afternoon in the 1880s watched the pilgrims who had crossed the water by a bridge of boats light their candles and hand them to the sacristan and his assistants. Placed beside the altar the candles formed a solid wall of embossed, flickering gold. Looking back into the body of the church he observed the peasants, wearing coloured woollen shirts and blue scarves round their waists, compose a symphony of blue, red and black checks. After the service a joyous *festa* continued till midnight.

Behind the high altar the choir, like the presbytery, is transverse to the main axis, but rectangular. The stalls are of seventeenth-century woodwork in the style of the Fleming Albert van der Brulle. They are splendidly carved, though heavy. On the ceiling are three roundels by Giuseppe Salviati, brought from Santo Spirito. On the walls above the stalls contemporary statues stand in niches between pilasters; those on the long end wall terminating, to the architect's satisfaction, the scenographical theme from one end of the basilica to the other.

The sacristy lying to the left of the choir is a picture gallery. Three vigorous ceiling panels by Titian, difficult to see, are under the influence of Michelangelo. In *The Sacrifice of Isaac* the terrified face of the little victim, his head bent to the ground by Abraham's beefy arm on his neck, is poignant. Altogether there are thirteen Titians in this room. On the rear wall to the left as you enter is his altarpiece of *St Mark Enthroned*, finished in 1510, the year in which Giorgione died and the artist's detachment from his influence became evident. The Evangelist is very magisterial, holding the open Gospel on his knee, between four saints of whom St Damian in a crimson robe in the forefront presents a splendid profile and St Sebastian wears the expression of someone to whom an indecent proposal has been made. Ruskin thought the picture was spoilt, but since his day it has been properly restored and cleaned so that the colours are now brilliant. Over the entrance are Pietro Liberi's *Last Supper* and Salviati's *David dodging the Lance hurled by Saul*. The marvellous fifteenth-century Flemish tapestry, the *Whitsunday Celebration*, from a cartoon by Giovanni Bellini, now does service as an altar frontal.

But the cream of the collection is Tintoretto's *Marriage at Cana*, dated 1551 and measuring some 27 feet long by 15 feet high. It was commissioned by the Crociferi Fathers for their refectory. Some of the assembled Apostles and women are said to be members of Tintoretto's family and friends. The company and surroundings certainly denote a prosperous bourgeois rather than patrician lot such as Veronese would have depicted. Indeed the scene and the figures are entirely profane, if we exclude the haloed Christ and his Mother seated beside him at the end of the table, looking, dare one say it, rather out of place amongst so much jollity. For one has only to take in the bustle and excitement of the party: the maid in a red coat and blue kerchief, unconscious of her beauty, proffering a bearded Apostle (Tintoretto himself) a glass bowl full of white wine; the maid on her right pouring a stream of liquid from a huge amphora into a more manageable vessel; and the manservant in the right foreground endeavouring with effort to lift another mammoth amphora. In the right background guests are still arriving, although where they will be seated remains a mystery. To the beamed ceiling are attached heavy metal brackets, from one of which a branched candelabrum with guttering candles is suspended, and from the others pennons which look like old stockings or seaweed fluttering in the breeze. From a range of upper windows on the left sunlight streams upon a row of ravishingly beautiful women, fair-complexioned and fair-haired, their heads bejewelled, their slender necks and open bosoms bare but for the occasional pearl choker. Although the Apostles are seated with their backs to the windows yet their faces are so turned that they too catch the sunlight, while throwing into partial shadow the dishes of fruit and the decanters on the brilliantly white table-cloth. At the furthest end of the room arched openings, against which groups of unidentified persons, some turbaned, some musicians, are standing, reveal an azure sky flecked with white clouds.

It is gratifying that Ruskin considered this painting, albeit smacking of the high Renaissance, one of the world's greatest works of art. Nevertheless he was surprised 'to find Tintoret, whose tone of mind was always grave, and who did not like to make a picture out of brocades and diadems, throwing his whole strength into the conception of a marriage feast'. He was pleased nevertheless that 'the mighty master' conformed to the academic rules of composition in his brilliant handling of masses and shadows. Ruskin called this painting 'sober and majestic in the highest degree', and 'perhaps the most perfect example which human art has produced of the utmost possible force and sharpness of shadow united with richness of local colour'.

It is interesting too that Ruskin, the redoubtable English professor of art, internationally renowned, to whom one would suppose doors would be thrown open which to ordinary mortals would remain closed, had occasion to complain of the officious and ignorant guide who persistently dogged him in the sacristy where he longed to be left in peace, and alone: 'The cicerone who escorts the stranger round the sacristy in the course of five minutes, and allows him some forty seconds for the contemplation of a picture which the study of six months would not entirely fathom, directs his attention very carefully to the "bell' effetto di prospettivo" of the long table.'

Today, mercifully, one is, no longer escorted at breakneck speed by a bored and impatient attendant. Instead, after a piercing click of warning, a deafening voice from the heavens as of Jehovah addressing Moses from Mount Sinai in something of a hurry, exclaims, '*Ullo! Ullo!* (for the benefit of foreign visitors unaccustomed to '*Pronto!*'), *Signori, Signore, questa bella sala contien' i più famosi e squisiti quadri del mondo*', followed by an enumeration of each item. At least the owner of the voice does not chase one out of the sacristy after forty seconds. One is allowed to take as long as one likes looking at the collection, provided one can ignore ten interruptions of that gruesome hiccough and Jehovah's sequel, '*Ullo! Ullo! Signori, Signore, questa bella sala . . .*'.

Work on the Salute proceeded slowly throughout the seventeenth century. By 1660 the Tirolean Thomas Ruer had placed the Four Evangelists on the façade and by 1663 Cavrioli's two sibyls and the Madonna were in place above the main entrance. At the end of October 1679 Longhena was drafting minor finishing touches to the church. By 1681 the interior was complete in every detail save a few prophets and allegories still in commission. On 9 November 1687 the solemn consecration took place. But Baldassare Longhena, sole author of the stupendous conception, was not there to witness it. He had died in 1682 at the age of fifty-one.

In 1806 the Somaschi Fathers were made to abandon the seminary, just as the Benedictines were chased out of San Giorgio Maggiore. On the fall of Napoleon in 1817 the Somaschi were allowed to return, re-occupy their old quarters and celebrate masses in the church as before.

PALAZZO or CA' REZZONICO

1660s – eighteenth century

Today we do not approach the Palazzo, or Ca' Rezzonico, as it is familiarly called, by water. Yet a few of its blue and white striped *pali* with urn-shaped tops and little gilded knobs still stand firmly before the fan of steps descending to the Grand Canal. On very special occasions like a public reception, gondolas are wont to wedge themselves within the space provided while disembarking or embarking privileged guests. The site of the Ca' Rezzonico is a prominent one on the Riva Destra, or right bank of the Grand Canal, if you are coming from the railway station. Being on a bend of the Canal it can be seen from the *vaporetto* landing-stage at San Tomà, and, if you are coming from St Mark's, from the Accademia stage. It can no longer be approached by the *traghetto* di San Samuele on the Riva Sinistra for the *traghetto* has lately been scrapped and replaced by the *vaporetto* stage of San Samuele. This stage is apt to be a snare and a delusion for few *vaporetti*, presumably the very slow ones, stop at it at all.

Nevertheless, it is worth looking at the Ca' Rezzonico across the water from the little Campo di San Samuele, of which two sides are bounded by the church with picturesque twelfth-century campanile, and the grand Palazzo Grassi. There is something village-like in a very grand palace adjacent to a church with campanile giving on to a small *campo* (the village green) and a canal (or artificial lake). Another such example beyond the Rialto Bridge is the Palazzo Labia and church of San Geremia. As for the Palazzo Grassi, it holds an interest for us in that it was built by the architect who completed the Ca' Rezzonico, and is a no less monumental building. Giorgio

Massari was Venice's leading architect of the first half of the eighteenth century. His masterpiece was the Gesuati church on the Zattere, its temple-like façade an adaptation of Palladio's San Giorgio Maggiore without the aisle wings. His compositions form a bridge from the Baroque to the Neo-classical style; indeed one might call them a reversion to the Palladian.

First of all, a brief word about the history of the Ca' Rezzonico. It was begun for a cultivated procurator of the city, the patrician Filippo Bon di San Barnabà, in 1667. Bon employed the great architect Baldassare Longhena. Nine years later another wealthy procurator, Leonardo Pesaro, commissioned Longhena to build a vast palace which still retains his name at San Stae. Although extremely impressive the Palazzo Pesaro is, as one might expect of that grandiloquent family, less restrained than the other. It is overfull of figures in the window spandrels and of grotesque heads on the waterline. The Ca' Rezzonico has, as Professor Lauritzen puts it, more *gravitas*.

The Ca' Rezzonico proved too expensive for the Procurator Bon and at the time of Longhena's death in 1682 only the ground floor and *piano nobile* were finished. Until the procurator's death in 1712 the palace remained incomplete. His heirs commissioned Massari to add the two upper floors; but they too found they had bitten off more than they could chew. In 1746 the palace was put in the market and sold to the extremely rich Genoese banker, Gian Battista Rezzonico, who re-commissioned Massari to continue work he had already begun for Filippo Bon.

The Rezzonico family originally came from Como and in 1687 got themselves admitted to the Libro d'Oro, or social register, on donating the mandatory 100,000 ducats to the Venetian treasury. In other words, the *nouveaux riches* Rezzonico had arrived. Their importance was assured, not merely by the completion and decoration of the most splendid palace in Venice but by the election in 1758 of Gian Battista's son, Carlo della Torre Rezzonico, Bishop of Padua, to the Holy See in succession to Pope Benedict XIV. Clement XIII was a good theologian and canonist. In the papal lights of the eighteenth century he lived modestly – he gave all his ecclesiastical revenues to the poor and the Church. Nevertheless he practised nepotism on a generous scale, creating two of his nephews cardinals and a third a Roman senator. Pope Clement was, in spite of the traditional ambivalence of Venice's relations with the papacy, delighted with the honour bestowed upon it. The Senate made all the Rezzonico males hereditary knights and advanced yet another nephew to the dignity of procurator. In return the grateful pontiff bestowed upon the Serene Republic the Golden Rose, which until the fall of the Republic in 1797 was kept in St Mark's treasury. On the whole, Clement was a good pope who endeavoured to be impartial in his relations with foreign powers and not to favour his beloved Venice unduly. When the whole of Europe was seeking to eliminate the Jesuits he defended them through thick and thin. He loved the arts and letters but his pudicity was excessive. He had the male organ of every statue in the Vatican collections provided with a fig leaf.

Pope Clement XIII was throughout his life greatly attached to the Palazzo Rezzonico. The rooms he occupied in the course of fleeting visits to Venice, while bishop of Padua, were on the mezzanine between the ground and first floors. The year of the pope's death, 1769, the Palazzo Rezzonico was made the scene of a sumptuous entertainment of Maria Theresa's son, the Emperor Joseph II. Lauritzen records that, 'One hundred young girls from four of the city's conservatoires serenaded him until 4 in the morning. Six hundred patricians were invited and one hundred and twenty richly dressed ladies added to the brilliance of the occasion.' But, alas, the young emperor, intensely serious-minded, was unmoved by feminine charms. As soon as his mother was dead and he was in full control of government he declared Austria independent of the pope and prohibited the publication of all papal bulls without his consent.

By 1810 the Rezzonico family had died out. Their day of glory and that of the palace, which had been fabulous, were over. They had employed the most famous artists of the mid-eighteenth century to embellish the state rooms – Giorgio Massari, Giovanni Battista Crosato, Andrea Brustolon,

Giambattista Tiepolo and his son, Domenico. They had created the most splendid and beautiful Baroque apartments in Venice. During the nineteenth century the palace changed hands. In 1837 kinsmen of the last Rezzonico sold the palace to a Pole, Ladislao Zselinski. In the 1880s it was bought by Pen Browning, the English poet Robert Browning's son, with his rich American wife's money. There exists a snapshot taken in 1889 of Pen standing beside his father at the water-gate. Both look crumpled and self-conscious. The poet leans against a rusticated pillar. He is gazing towards the Accademia. With his long white beard he appears hale and hearty, although by the end of that year he would be dead. Pen wears a small bowler hat turned up at the brims. His jaunty attitude does not deceive us into mistaking that he made a great success of life; nor do his small beady eyes or dapper moustache inspire great confidence.

The last private owner was the Venetian antiquarian Baron Hirschel de Minerbi. In 1931 the Ca' Rezzonico was bought by the commune. In 1936 it was opened as the city's museum of eighteenth-century decorative arts. The decorations, the frescoes and painted ceilings of the principal rooms were, with few exceptions, already there. But nearly all the present contents were either acquired or brought to the palace by the Civico Museo Correr. The administrators of that museum have contrived one of the most successful make-believes of a patrician dwelling not merely in Venice but the whole of Italy.

There is in existence an oil painting (*circa* 1730) by Canaletto of the Grand Canal looking towards the projecting Palazzo Balbi in the middle foreground. In the left foreground appears in perspective the Ca' Rezzonico as Longhena left it, that is to say ground floor and *piano nobile* capped by a sort of makeshift pediment covering the entire roof space. There also exists an elevation engraving by the Friar P. V. M. Coronelli (published in the second tome of *La Singolarità di Venezia* in 1708) of the two-floor building in exactly the same condition. Neither shows the unfinished palazzo in an attractive guise. There is yet another elevation engraving by Coronelli showing the palazzo as Longhena intended it, with some differences of detail from what we see now. To begin with, Longhena meant the deeply channelled rustication of the ground floor to have four arches instead of the three existing lintelled openings in the centre. Instead of the pairs of windows resting on fat consoles at either end as now, the engraving shows two pairs of rectangular windows lighting the mezzanine floor with smaller square windows below them. On the first and second floors four central bays are shown separated from the two end bays by coupled columns, whereas now the arcades of the two floors are unbroken, in the manner of Sansovino's Marcian Library. In other respects Massari followed Longhena's design fairly faithfully, down to the sculpture. Even the pretty reclining *putti* over the windows of the first floor, by the Fleming Josse de Corte, are like most of the sculptured keystones – definitely part of Longhena's theme – repeated on the top floor.

The whole façade is of stone trundled across the Gulf of Venice from Istria. The projecting parts are white, and the receding parts black. The stone of the upper floors is generally whiter than that of the bottom floor. The façade is returned on both sides by one bay, according to custom. Since the south side overlooking the Rio de San Barnabà is more conspicuous than the other, so it is more finished. Nevertheless, careful scrutiny will reveal that the sculptural detail, being more classical than Baroque in feeling, belongs to Massari's regime. It is serener if not more austere. The rest of the long south front consists of plain pink-washed walls divided into panels by horizontal string courses. The windows are grouped in couples and the beautifully carved masks on the keystones stand out against the unadorned background. Or rather the female heads on the top storey are clean and distinguishable whereas the helmeted and plumed heads of the males on the *piano nobile* are black and all but indistinguishable.

And what impression did the Ca' Rezzonico make on nineteenth-century art historians and men of letters? They did not like it much; yet they could not ignore so vast, so ponderous an edifice (*'maestoso mole'* as the Italian guide books call it) on a conspicuous site of the Grand Canal. John Ruskin in *The Stones of Venice* dismissed it succinctly as 'of the Grotesque Renaissance time, but less extravagant than usual'. Well, that was fairly flattering from him. By grotesque he meant Baroque, a style he could not be expected to be enthusiastic about. 'The Renaissance palaces', he went on, referring now to all those which came after the medieval,

> are not more picturesque in themselves than the clubhouses of Pall Mall [those which have been suffered to remain by a later generation, like The Travellers' and The Reform, are universally admired today]; but they become delightful by the contrast of their severity and refinement with the rich and rude confusion of the sea-life beneath them, and of their white and solid masonry with the green waves. Remove from beneath them the orange sails of the fishing boats, the black gilding of the gondolas, the cumbered decks and rough crews of the barges of traffic, and the fretfulness of the green water along their foundations, and the Renaissance palaces possess no more interest than those of London or Paris. But the Gothic palaces are picturesque in themselves, and wield over us an independent power. Sea and sky, and every other accessory, might be taken from them, and they would be beautiful and strange.

Ruskin was understandably fascinated by the ever varying, lapping water-line of these edifices growing out of the water, when on the passing of large craft the waves disclosed barnacles, seaweed and marine slime clinging to the massive foundations and momentarily stripped them of their subaqueous secrets.

Henry James was no less entranced. He referred to the Ca' Rezzonico as, 'This great seventeenth-century pile, thrusting itself upon the water with a peculiar florid assurance, a certain upward toss of its cornice which gives it the air of a rearing sea-horse, decorates immensely – and within, as well as without – the wide angle that it commands.' The image of the sea-horse prancing and snorting to attract attention is a happy one, for truly these palaces are never static owing to the ceaseless movement of the Canal. Yet on paper the Venetian Baroque façades appear just as staid and tame as the Roman palace elevations of the same period and style; and compared to the

Bavarian and Austrian counterparts, positively ponderous. Because of the water they become animate things, for ever shifting, agitating, restless and disturbed, as though awaiting anxiously the last trump to summon the terrible convulsion which must one future day surely rise and swallow them up unprotesting. James with that disarming grin of self-disparagement, which one interprets as one dares, goes on to protest that

> doubts and fears course rapidly through my mind – I am easily their victim when it is a question of architecture – as they are apt to do today in Italy, almost anywhere, in the presence of the beautiful, of the desecrated or the neglected. We feel at such moments as if the eye of Mr. Ruskin were upon us; we grow nervous and lose our confidence. This makes me inevitably, in talking of Venice, seek a pusillanimous safety in the trivial and the obvious.

Let this also be my humble excuse faced with the scholars of my generation, the Wittkowers, Clarks, Lorenzettis, Lauritzens and Honours.

There is only one way for you – and me – to get into the palace, and that is by the Fondamenta running between the garden of the palace and the Rio di San Barnabà. It is one of those hundreds of Venetian cul-de-sacs which end in nothing – in this case water.

On your left through cracks in the temporary fence you catch a glimpse of a deserted garden at the rear of the palace. You sense that only a short time ago this garden was larger than it is now. Patches of green are as valuable as emeralds in Venice, and far more desirable. The scruffiest little trees and the coarsest grasses should be treasured. But it seems as though this fragmentary patch is no longer part of the precincts. A noble Baroque portal with curved and broken pediment, now barricaded and barred, and guarded by the head of a venerable greybeard on the keystone, evidently gave access to it. It is not fanciful to attribute the portal to Longhena. But by whom is the figure of Our Lady standing on the wall to the left of the portal? Her stone garments flutter whether there is a breeze or not, and her haloed head is protected by a pretty parasol of green metal with a frilly border.

A few steps further and you reach the entrance to the palace. A passage leads you to a vestibule with a niched fountain proudly displaying the Rezzonico armorial shield in marble. Any other Venetian family – if we except the Pesaro – would have had a more modest one. Before it an enclosed courtyard once formed part of the garden. You are in the great atrium of the water-gate with the Grand Canal at the far end, seen through the three intercolumns. All is dank and dark. A monumental stairway with shallow steps takes you to the *piano nobile*. The peach marble walls are panelled in a jazzy pattern of raised moulds in stone. High casemented windows with fans light the well. The peach ceiling is deeply coved. On the fat stone newels of the stairs two horrid little *putti* doff their caps. They represent Autumn and Winter, and are signed by Josse de Corte. Since the monumental staircase was, like the great ballroom, to which it leads, an addition by Massari, these coarse statuettes must have been left-overs from Longhena's workshop. The staircase is essentially Longhenaesque and recalls the seventeenth-century master's *scalone* at San Giorgio Maggiore.

The Rezzonico were so rich and grand that a ballroom, or Salone delle Feste, of vast dimensions was needed for entertainments. Projected over the space between two pre-existing wings this *chef d'oeuvre* of Massari takes in the height of two storeys. In 1755 walls and ceiling were entirely frescoed in *trompe-l'oeil* by Giovanni Battista Crosato with the help of Pietro Visconti, one of Tiepolo's collaborators. Crosato was a Venetian whose works for the house of Savoy, highly esteemed in his day, '*sont oubliés aujourd'hui*' (as Bénézit puts it in a disparaging aside). On the contrary this prolific artist, not admittedly of the highest order, but capable, left memorable and charming frescoes in the Palazzo Stupinighi, the Villa Regina, the Palazzo Reale and a number of churches in Turin; and did much to transform Piedmontese decorative painting. His enlistment by the Rezzonico gives some indication of that family's ambitions.

On walking into the Salone delle Feste you are immediately confronted by a great shield of the Ca' Rezzonico over a feigned cornice. Feigned martial figures are painted to stand between feigned giant columns of wave blue and feigned pilasters with gilded capitals supporting a gilded entablature, likewise feigned. The ceiling allegory is an apotheosis of the Rezzonico family in the four parts of the world. The gypsum pavement is the colour of gooseberry fool. As becomes a ballroom, the furniture is sparse and arranged against the walls. It consists of a suite carved in boxwood by Andrea Brustolon, the greatest joiner of the Italian Rococo who was also a sculptor of note. The backs and seats of the armchairs are upholstered in petit point. The arms and legs of the chairs are minutely carved to resemble gnarled tree branches, supported by tiny Moorish slaves of ebony. Gueridons in the shape of naked negroes with boxwood chains round their necks, and a large and intricate vase-stand incorporating gods of mythology form part of this suite which belonged to the Venier family. The remainder of the suite is found in Room XII, entered by a door on the left. According to John Fleming and Hugh Honour's *Dictionary of Decorative Arts*, Brustolon made this exquisite furniture before he returned to his native Belluno in 1699. The ballroom is illuminated by an immense candelabrum of wood and gilded metal, sole remnants of such fittings from the time of Longhena.

By 1762 the Salone delle Feste was ready for a princely reception in celebration of Ludovico Rezzonico's nomination to the procuratorship; and two years later for a ball, attended by the whole nobility of Venice, given in honour of the Duke of York, brother of King George III of Great Britain.

The adjacent room over the Rio di San Barnabà is the Sala dell'Allegoria Nuziale, called after the magnificent ceiling by Giambattista Tiepolo which celebrates the marriage of Ludovico Rezzonico to Faustina Savorgnan of an ancient and noble family. Tiepolo was working here in 1758, having returned from Würzburg where he was engaged on the stupendous staircase ceiling of the archiepiscopal palace. The bridal pair are drawn by a pair of white stallions in the chariot of the sun, accompanied by Apollo and preceded by a blindfold Cupid carrying a torch and releasing a dove of peace. The scene is enacted in an effulgence of light, rendered the more sparkling by the sombre red damask wall hangings. From this Sala an oratory is literally suspended over the *rio*. It is a pretty little closet with Rococo walls of white and grey stucco.

A small internal staircase leads from the Sala to the mezzanine below. Here Pope Clement lodged in the eighteenth century and Robert Browning died in one of the rooms on 12 December 1889. It is dedicated to the poet's memory, being supplied with a few of his books and relics and some simple furniture of his period. For many years however the mezzanine has been firmly shut and no admission allowed.

The Ca' Rezzonico belonged to the poet's son, Pen Browning. Mrs Bronson recorded that the father in his last years had set his mind on acquiring for himself and his sister the Palazzo Manzoni, a huge building much in need of restoration. Nothing would make him heed his friends' remonstrances. Until his last months he enjoyed robust health and took long walks in Venice and on the Lido. He vastly enjoyed visiting bric-à-brac shops and buying old tapestries and carved furniture which he would carry home by gondola in transports of triumph. He loved the Venetian people, would talk to them on his walks and play with their children. When the statue of Carlo Goldoni was erected in the Campo di San Bartolomeo in 1883 he wrote, at the mayor of Venice's request, a sonnet to mark the occasion. He was extremely popular with the citizens and commune.

To his friends' relief purchase of the Palazzo Manzoni fell through, and so he consented to live with Pen and his wife in the Ca' Rezzonico. The size of the palace did not daunt him in the least. In November 1889 he wrote, 'What strikes me as most noteworthy is the cheerfulness and comfort of the huge rooms. The building is warmed throughout by a furnace and pipes.' Nevertheless two days before he died Pen and his wife, aware of the poet's deteriorating condition, moved themselves and him to the entresol between the *piano nobile* and the ground floor, so that he might pass into the dining-room without strain. When Browning died his draped coffin lay in state in the long but low Portego di Mezzo on the *piano nobile*. It was photographed in front of the grand doorway, on either side of which a pair of Persian statues supported globes with their hands and heads. The globes having gone, the Persians now bend beneath the weight of nothing. The coffin was duly carried by eight stalwart *pompieri* (firemen) in uniform to the highly decorated municipal barge, then towed reverently by a steam launch with glowing torches to the chapel on the island of San Michele. Pen had placed a wreath of laurel leaves on the bier. Thence two days later it was transported to the railway station for England. Robert Browning was buried in Westminster Abbey on 31 December.

From the Sala dell'Allegoria Nuziale one enters what is now called the Sala dei Pastelli on account of the fine series of pictures by Rosalba and G. A. Lazzari. Above tomato damask walls and curtains to match is another ceiling by Crosato, *The Apotheosis of Poetry*. Through the Sala degli Arazzi (Flemish tapestries against greeny yellow walls of holland and ceiling frescoed by Jacopo Guarana) the Throne Room is reached, at the angle where the little Rio di San Barnabà joins the Grand Canal. The walls of this room are hung with deep wine patterned velvet, and the ceiling is the second to be painted by Giambattista Tiepolo with the theme of Merit between Nobility and Virtue. Again the same perspective effects, and colours of the same sparkling clarity.

The name of this room derives from the great throne and *baldacchino* erected for Pope Pius VI on his return to Rome from Vienna, where he had gone to combat the Emperor Joseph II's Erastian edicts against the authority of the Church. The meeting between emperor and pope proved abortive, a sort of Canossa in reverse, although the pope received much sympathy and a great welcome from the Austrians. In the Palazzo Rezzonico he broke his silence. In pretending that the visit had been successful he implied that a concordat with Austria was forthcoming. In fact it came to nothing. The papal throne is elaborately carved and gilded. On the long inner wall hangs a full-length portrait of Pietro Barbarigo of the dogal family, painted by Bernardino Castelli in the early second half of the eighteenth century. The be-wigged and berobed nobleman standing before a background of tasselled drapery has been given the most enormous Baroque frame, adorned with allegorical figures, *putti*, keys and implements of all sorts under a towering crest which embraces the subject's armorial shield. If not actually carved by Antonio Corradini, maker of the last *bucintoro* (or doges' barge), it undoubtedly comes from his workshop. The rest of the rich furniture in the Throne Room is his. Highly ornate, over-wrought and over-gilded, Corradini's carved furniture took Venice by storm and inspired young William Kent from England to design when he got home sofas, chairs and writing-tables in what he believed to be the same genre, but was in fact far less sophisticated and consequently more beautiful.

From the Sala degli Arazzi is reached the Portego di Mezzo, to which I have already referred. This long, rectangular apartment, or rather passageway, is lit by the three central windows overlooking the Grand Canal and three overlooking the courtyard at the rear. It has a plain ceiling of transverse beams, walls of green feigned marble and four niches for busts, of which two are signed by Vittoria.

The Portego di Mezzo, a gallery, divides the Ca' Rezzonico axially into two halves. On the far side and in the north-east corner of the palace, overlooking the Grand Canal, the Sala del Tiepolo is named after the third ceiling by Giambattista. It was painted on canvas in 1744–5 for the Palazzo Barbarigo at Santa Maria del Giglio and transported here. The subject, *Strength and Knowledge*, is one of the master's most ethereal, luminous and iridescent paintings. In this room are samples of much vaunted Venetian Baroque furniture, notably the walnut *bureau-trumeau*, with florid and top-heavy crest over a panel of engraved Venetian glass. When treated like architecture and overloaded with a concentration of statuettes, shields and crockets Baroque furniture can too often be overpowering, and even ugly.

On this north side of the Portego di Mezzo is the Library, with a heavy ceiling of which the ground colour is lilac. Over-gilded compartments contain five mythological paintings by Francesco Maffei, a contemporary of Longhena. A native of Vicenza he was an unorthodox painter who discarded the shackles of current academic influences to develop a character-istic brush stroke, free and unrestrained. The deep cornice is, like the bookcases, of mahogany. The latter are likewise treated architecturally, with segmental pediments carried by fluted pilasters. The walls are wainscoted to the tops of the presses. It is a dark, gloomy room.

An unimpressive staircase with simple barrel vault leads to the second floor. You debouch straight into the Portego dei Dipinti, which is what the name implies, a gallery of interesting pictures, mostly eighteenth-century. They are just the sort of paintings one would expect to find in a private palace of this date, size and importance. They are however part of the collection of the Civico Museo Correr. They cannot all be mentioned. G. B. Piazzetta's *Death of Darius* is remarkable for its highlights. Piazzetta belongs to that group of three (Sebastiano Ricci and Giambattista Tiepolo) responsible for a resurgence of Venetian painting in the early eighteenth century, after the appreciable decline in the standard of Venetian painting during the *seicento*. It was the fault of the patrician patrons who had become extremely rich, conservative and unadventurous. They clung to the illusion that they were the representatives of a world power which in actual fact was in decline. The artists they liked to employ were out of date and safe; they would not venture with the avant-garde or even the young. Both Sebastiano and Marco Ricci had to seek patronage abroad; and at first even Tiepolo found commissions more readily in Udine and Germany, but not for long. The fancifulness and gaiety of his designs, the sparkle of his colours, the lightness of his touch, combined with the ability to treat archaic themes with a refined and polished elegance verging on the slick, somewhat in the manner with which Rex Whistler learned to beguile English squires in the 1930s, captivated the old Venetian aristocrats. They soon tumbled over one another in prevailing upon him to immortalize them on ceilings and walls in the guise of Apollo or Mars, and their wives in the role of Cleopatra or Diana. Witness the glowing examples which the Rezzonico and Labia families have left us in their respective palaces.

It is questionable how far these millionaire socialites appreciated the virtuosity of his technique, the mastery of his perspective effects, which were revolutionary, and the play of his imagination which was supra-mundane. Francis Haskell has pointed out that Tiepolo's themes transcended the usual run of Rococo frivolity and eroticism almost exclusively favoured at this time by the patrons of Boucher, Watteau and Fragonard in France. He chose the nobler scenes of Roman culture and war. What Tiepolo brought to Venice owed little to his suave *seicento* predecessors, and nothing to his contemporaries. It came, apart from his own fertile imagination, from a lifelong study of the *cinquecento* Veronese, and fed upon the pretensions of his extravagant patrons.

In the Portego dei Dipinti a dreadful picture of *St Philip Neri taking Communion* by Giuseppe Angeli gives one a turn; the head does not belong to the body. *The View of a Bridge over a River* with foreground figures on the quay attributed to Luca Carlevaris, the portrait of *Cardinal Federico Corner* by Strozzi, *The Interior of St Peter's* by Panini and *The Rio dei Mendicanti* by Canaletto all take my fancy, on the other hand.

The first of a series of small rooms on this floor along the Rio di San Barnabà is the Sala dei Longhi. Here are gathered no less than thirty paintings by this master of high and low life, the Venetian Hogarth. Among the important collection is a portrait, rather like a Goya, of Tiepolo's brother-in-law, Francesco Guardi, in undress, with open neck and ruffled sleeves. Grey curls from a bag-wig fall upon his left shoulder. It is a charming likeness of a highly observant and satirical artist, who lived at a time when the Venetian people seemed to indulge lives of perpetual carnival. Yellow-painted lacquer tables and chairs are ranged against walls hung with plain yellow stuff edged with lacquered borders. The ceiling of this splendid room, the fourth by Tiepolo, displays *The Triumph of Zephyrus* brought from the Palazzo Pesaro. Because the ceiling is low and light is reflected from the *rio* the painting can be seen clearly and easily. The god of the west wind wearing gigantic dragon-fly wings is in process of abducting Flora, who is naked but for an orange garment with blue ribbons loosely attached to her waist. With his right arm the amorous god enfolds her and with his left he raises aloft a wreath of flowers.

Next is the Green Lacquer Room. The walls by contrast are

hung with ravishing silk panels, predominantly green, in a pattern of bold Rococo squirls and roses, like a Chinese paper. A huge Baroque mirror with flaming crest of gilt foliage reflects in the ancient lead-tinted glass a complete suite of green and gold lacquer chairs, commodes and tripod stands. The backs and seats of the chairs are covered with the same patterned silk as the walls. This famous room from the Palazzo Calbo-Crotta agli Scalzi was brought and re-erected here by the Civico Museo Correr. Even the ceiling, *The Triumph of Diana* by Guardi, is part of the transported *salotto*. The goddess, spear in hand, crescent moon hovering above her head, bends forward from her precarious cloud to pat a hound which is being hugged rather than upheld in mid air by a loving *putto*. The pictures are eighteenth-century topographical views of Venice.

The third room of this series is the Sala del Guardi. Within irregular oval frames of stucco are three monochrome or faded frescoes by Guardi of *Minerva*, *Apollo* and *Venice* personified, taken from the Palazzo Dabalà for which they were executed. The fourth room is the Camera dell'Alcova, brought from the Palazzo Carminati at Stae. The pretty sepia wall paper is a fanciful, repetitive pattern of the Arch of Titus, Rome. The bed cover is in shreds caused by over-exposure to light. Over it hangs a pastel by Rosalba of the *Madonna and Child*. Under glass is exhibited a toilet service of 58 pieces in bronze and silver gilt made in Augsburg for the Pisani-Grimani family. Through the bedroom two little 'cabinets' are reached – the Camerino del Falchetto, called after the ceiling fresco of a falcon in flight by Gian Domenico Tiepolo; and the enchanting Camerino degli Stucchi, its walls and ceiling in painted stucco work of branches and flowers with mirrors inset in the curved corners. It comes from the Palazzo Calbo-Crotta. It is a rare work of art and the best of its kind left in Venice. One would pronounce it incomparable had the re-painting not been so indifferently done.

Our surfeit of art and decoration is not quite over. You are obliged to cross the Portego dei Dipinti to the north wing of the second floor, for here are to be found the enchanting caricature frescoes of Domenico, Giambattista's son and pupil. The series of rooms called la Villa di Zianigo contains frescoes transferred to canvas and brought entire from a small house which belonged to Tiepolo father and son near Mira, and was demolished in this century. The first room, No. XX, is the entrance hall, the walls depicting Rinaldo swooning before the comical statue of Armida. It is the poorest fresco of the lot. You pass through a small, windowless passage room, called Portego del Mondo Nuovo, and approach the backviews of a group of people gazing out to sea. They are concentrating upon the mysterious future. There is the familiar pierrot in a white conical cap; a man on a stool balancing a long stick; a peasant woman with a basket on the ground; and a pig-tailed gentleman waving his tricorne hat.

The rest of the frescoes are in this vein, a sort of *capriccio* cycle in which the people (*il Mondo Nuovo*) mingle with the nobility in scenes carnavalesque and mythological. Although much damaged they represent one of the most delightful and popular aspects of Domenico's work. They comprise three monochrome panels feigning stucco in high relief of centaurs, satyrs, and fauns dancing. Two of the scenes in fresco are called *The Minuet in the Villa* and *Three People out Walking*, in which the artist is poking fun at the fashion for classical decoration of gods and goddesses and the absurdly exaggerated styles of dress in the last decades of the eighteenth century. Domenico has caught and arrested for ever rich and poor in attitudes cheerful and melancholy, pompous and absurd, and even touching. In *La Passeggiata à Tre* he makes a stout lady in a yellow dress bunched at the waist, and wearing a full white bonnet tied at the back of her head in a blue bow, walk away from us with an admirer at either arm, one wearing a tricorne, the other a tall hat, with a whippet dog beside him. La Camera dei Pagliacci contains the famous ceiling fresco of the masked buffoons performing acrobatics on stretched ropes. They swing, they turn somersaults, they gossip and, more poignantly, they lie on the ground exhausted by their antics, or simply make love. The tiny chapel by contrast has a monochrome panel of boys devoutly saying the rosary before an altar. The subject of the ceiling is still more solemn: *Deeds in the life of St Jerome Emiliani*, founder of the Clerks Regular of Somaschi and patron saint of orphans. It was painted by Domenico before the other rooms, when he was barely twenty-two.

Leaving the Villa di Zianigo by the entrance hall you pass into la Sala della Spinetta, named after the eighteenth-century inlaid instrument, the sides painted with pastoral and hunting scenes. It is supported by three very clumsy legs. Two steps up and you are in a corridor which makes a kink in order to bypass the staircase. In it hangs a small pastoral landscape by Zuccharelli as scintillating as a Guardi. The latter artist happens to be represented here by one of four paintings illustrating the art of the devotional crown makers. A few steps down and you are in the Sala del Ridotto (or gaming resort), overlooking the Grand Canal. Ceiling and cove are entirely covered by *The Triumph of Virtue* by Girolamo Mengozzi-Colonna, which is nothing special and shows the marks of the ceiling beams through the fresco. But the paintings which give their name to the room are Guardi's masterpieces, *Il Ridotto* and *Il Parlatorio*. In the former the most frequented room of a gaming house is shown, 'with its heavy air of corruption' as the TCI guidebook puts it. A man disguised by a domino is bowing low, presumably in derision, to a young woman, the upper part of whose face is masked, but whose despair is expressed by her attitude and gestures. At her side a black dwarf teases her little dog. In *Il Parlatorio* another young woman, undisguised, in the full flush of beauty, youth and affluence is in her turn playing with the same little dog before the grilles of the convent of San Zaccaria, which was a favourite meeting place of high Venetian society. Two well dressed youths in the foreground are looking up at a Punch and Judy show. Both paintings are brimful of vivacity, colour and rather sinister undertones. The Sala del Ridotto is furnished with a suite of yellow-painted armchairs and two commodes.

The third floor under Massari's roof contains some fascinating reconstructions of dismantled shops (a pharmacy among them), collections of porcelain and lacquer, costumes and a marionette theatre. But these things cannot all be seen in one visit to the Ca' Rezzonico. As it is there is scarcely a stool in the palace on which one is allowed to rest one's weary limbs. On my last visit there was a welcome notice at the bottom of the last flight of stairs – 'Closed'. A sigh of relief escaped me.

I GESUITI
(Santa Maria Assunta)

1714–29

The church of the Gesuiti must not be confused with the church of the Gesuati which is on the Zattere facing the Giudecca and is the ecclesiastical masterpiece of Giorgio Massari who completed the Ca' Rezzonico. Both churches, now eighteenth-century, were of medieval foundation and built for different religious orders, long since departed. The Gesuati never belonged to the Jesuits but to a thirteenth-century establishment inhabited by '*i poveri Gesuati*', meaning the poor followers of Jesus. When Massari came on the scene his clients were the Dominicans; and the Dominican fathers are still there. The history of the Gesuiti is very different; so too is its locality at the north-western end of the Fondamenta Nuove.

The occupants of the original church of Santa Maria Assunta on the site of the Gesuiti had been since the twelfth century the Crociferi, or Cross-bearers. They were an Order, confined to Italy, which was founded in Bologna to tend the sick and wounded – stretcher-bearers no less. They bore a distinguishing cross on their habit. Twice they were expelled and their property confiscated, the government allowing church, oratory and hospital, a nondescript block adjacent to the south side of the church, to be purchased by the Society of Jesus in 1657. Not that the Jesuits were popular in Venice. In 1606 they had been dismissed by the doge under pressure from the redoubtable Fra Paolo Sarpi in retaliation for Pope Paul V having put the Serene Republic under an interdict over a dispute concerning church property. In fact the audacity of this action against the pope's front line, so to speak, brought the papacy acute humiliation. John Julius Norwich tells the story. A terrible truth had to be faced. 'The interdict had failed. The most dread weapon in the papal armoury – that same weapon, the very threat of which in the Middle Ages was enough to bring kings and emperors to their knees – had lost its power. Worse, its failure had been revealed to the world.' Venice was flagrantly defying the interdict. She was creating a dreadful precedent. She was making it universally clear that nations and individuals need henceforth have no fear of excommunications. The Jesuits were re-admitted reluctantly after half a century of exile. Then, over a hundred years later, the society was totally suppressed, on the urgent demands of France, Spain, Portugal and several Italian states, by the submissive Pope Clement XIV in 1773. Again the Jesuits disappeared from Venice. In 1807 their monastery was turned into a barracks, not to be reconstituted until 1925. In 1844 however the Jesuits returned to their church and adapted some buildings at the entrance of the *salizada* for a new and humbler monastery.

It may seem surprising that the Jesuits, who felt obliged to keep a fairly low profile while they were allowed to be in Venice, nevertheless built a church in flamboyant style and at enormous cost. The answer is that like the Friars in the fourteenth century they always had extremely rich patrons and benefactors with cultivated tastes, many of whose younger sons joined the Society. These noble families were determined to build for the Society on traditionally lavish lines. Francis Haskell has pointed out that 'the general effect [of the Gesuiti] is one of very great wealth but absolute anonymity'. That is to say the paintings, sculptures and emblems without and within the Gesuiti church do not draw specific attention to the saints and glories of the Society. If taken over by another Order or merely turned into a *parocchiale*, the church would pass muster without the necessity for removing or obliterating proselytizing images.

So the Fathers were persuaded to rebuild their church in 1714. There is no reason to assume that their ambitions were pitched high. But no matter what the views of the Fathers were, their patrons saw to it that nothing second best would do either for the credit of their protégés, or for that matter of themselves. The exorbitantly rich Manin family were responsible for the most showy parts of the Gesuiti, namely the façade, the high altar, all the marble incrustations of the interior, the organ, the presbytery, the pavement, the ceilings, the statuary and the gilded stucco work which abounds. And they paid for these embellishments. The Manin were a comparatively new family from Udine who rose to prominence in the eighteenth century, bought themselves nobility and finally supplied to Venice her Doge Ludovico Manin, who surrendered to Napoleon in 1797. It seems that the Manin family were from the start consumed by a sort of *folie de grandeur*. The number of villas (notably Passeriano, approached by colonnades vying with St Peter's) and churches in Venetia, which they bought, or built, and filled with works of art, were almost legion. The architect they particularly favoured was Domenico Rossi, a Swiss of little education who was given to wild debaucheries. It was Rossi who based the plan of the Gesuiti on that of the prototype Jesuit church, the Gesù in Rome, namely a Latin cross of one nave and interconnecting side chapels.

Rossi, too young to have been a pupil of Longhena, was nevertheless influenced by him in that his building designs combine a linear severity with a sculptural overlay that produce high lights and deep shadows. His San Stae church of 1709, although evincing indisputably Baroque features, such as the ponderous, broken pediment of the central door and the plethora of sculpture, preserves the discipline of Palladio in the triumphal arch motif and the interplay of a lesser within a giant order of the façade. One senses that Rossi at San Stae was a reluctant baroquist, who would have been happier living and working either before or after his own age, in other words in Palladian or Neo-classical times.

But first the façade of the Gesuiti by Giambattista Fattoretto, of whom little is known. It is certainly one of the most lively in Venice. Basically it is modelled on the Gesù façade, that is to say divided into two stages of orders, the upper crowned by a pediment. Its difference to the Mannerist Gesù however lies in

the fact that the lower order is composed of eight huge
Corinthian columns carrying an entablature advanced and
recessed in full Baroque movement. The columns flank niches
with statues. The upper order is of more static and sober
design, like that of the prototype Gesù. Yet sobriety is certainly
not the keynote because of the galaxy of statues which jostle
together wherever there is space available for them. They are
just as saucily alive as the green vegetation and saplings which
sprout from the cracks of entablature and pediment. The
twelve Apostles and angels represented have appeared to many
writers as about to ascend into the skies in exaltation. For
instance, W. D. Howells wrote that 'the sight of those theatrical
angels, with their shameless, unfinished backs, flying off the top
of the rococo façade of the church of the Jesuits, has always
been a spectacle to fill me with despondency and foreboding'.

To my mind these statues look more like lost souls about to
throw themselves in despair to the bottomless pit, only
prevented from doing so by the rusted iron bands which tie
their loose limbs together and keep them in place. The
'despondency' Howells talks about seems to be theirs rather
than mine. James Morris complained that if you look behind
the angels on the portico you find that their buttocks are
hollow. It made him feel uncomfortable. Actually they are flat,
as are their backs, necks and heads. This fact induces in me a
fear that all the weight being in their fronts must sooner or later
topple them over. In any event they do not merit close scrutiny
with the exception of the predominant statue of the *Assunta* by
Giuseppe Torretto. She really is meant to be taking wing from
the apex of the pediment.

The interior of the Gesuiti is so amazing that at first one can
scarcely believe one's eyes. What I have written about Rossi at
San Stae seems inapplicable for here he has abandoned himself
to a riot of Rococo. It is interesting to read what arbiters of taste
throughout the ages thought of it. The mid-eighteenth century
Charles de Brosses found the architecture of the Gesuiti
passable within and without; he called the ceiling magnificent
and the tabernacle and baldaquin of the high altar beautiful;
and he greatly admired the Turkey carpet of marble. To the

nineteenth-century Ruskin however the interior represented, as we would expect, everything that he held in profoundest contempt. It is astonishing how this Victorian sage influenced cultivated taste, not merely in his own country, but throughout Europe and America for three-quarters of a century. The influence can be dated from the publication of *The Seven Lamps of Architecture* in 1849, followed by the first volume of *The Stones of Venice* in 1851. Théophile Gautier, who died in 1872, already touched by the Ruskin wand, was even more scathing; he was vitriolic on the subject of every Venetian Baroque church. He referred to

> its volutes, as tortuous as Joseph Prudhomme's* signature, its puffy cherubs, its castrated angels, its cartouches, which appear to need the barber's trim, its endive-shaped ornaments, overblown like cabbages, its unhealthy preciosities and its unbridled ornamentation which is akin to the excrescences of diseased stone; for all this we have developed an insuperable aversion. We are more than displeased, we are revolted. Nothing, in our opinion, could be further from the Christian ethic than this squalid hotch-potch of pious knick-knacks, than this luxury without beauty or grace, excessive and encumbered like a contractor's notebook, thanks to which the chapel of the Holy Virgin Mary could be mistaken for the boudoir of an Opera chorus-girl.

One wonders how so intellectual a writer could bring himself to be totally dismissive of a whole phase of art. One can only feel sad that he missed so much pleasure in his sightseeing. Gradually in the twentieth century did vitriol give way to less positive disapproval. J. G. Links quotes Murray's reference to the 'extraordinary specimen of the theatrical and luxurious', which is a degree less pejorative than Major Douglas's 'wealth only equalled by the vulgarity and bad taste displayed in the use of it' (1925).

The walls of the entire church are made of *verde antico* inlay on slabs of white marble, imitating a damask pattern from floor to

Joseph Prudhomme is a fictional character created by a satirical writer, Henri Monnier (b. 1805), who is described as an inept, self-satisfied petit-bourgeois who spouts inanities in solemn, sententious phrases.

ceiling. A deep gilded valance in relief hangs over the damask walls. The effect is convincing and dazzling. W. D. Howells while admitting that the workmanship was skilful and costly (which it is, and was intended to be) depreciated it thus:

> it only gives the church the effect of being draped in damask linen; and even where the marble is carved in vast and heavy folds over the pulpit to simulate a curtain, or wrought in figures on the steps of the high-altar to represent a carpet, it has no richness of effect, but a poverty, a coldness, a harshness indescribably table-clothy.

He called the Gesuiti 'a dreary sanctuary'. How could this jolly American consul be so disapproving of a building calculated to bring beauty and pleasure to a congregation in a poor district who feasted their eyes and senses on the splendour and luxury which they regarded as theirs? Because he was writing after 1850 – actually in 1867. Because he felt obliged by the great dictator of taste to equate splendour with wickedness and architectural trickery with moral degeneration. Had the Gesuiti been a nobleman's ballroom he might have conceded some merit to its lavish glitter. As it was he ought to have seen it for what it was intended, a pleasure dome for the Almighty's as well as his worshippers' delight. For some reason the enchanting pulpit came in for more animadversion than any other feature of the church. That God's holy word should be preached from a rostrum which was so utterly false and deceitful, masquerading as something which it wasn't, namely bunched and draped damask curtains, silken valance and dangling tassels, all of marble, manifested a sort of material confutation of the spiritual truths enunciated by the lips of an ordained priest standing in it.

We must bear in mind that when the Gesuiti was finished and its marvels were revealed in 1729 – for it took only fourteen years in building and decorating – its condition was fresher, brighter than today's. Although this huge church is constantly being patched it always has had, since I have known it, a somewhat seedy air. One longs to get a step-ladder and dust the canopy of the pulpit and the globe of the tabernacle, sponge down the statues within reach and even polish the damask walls. As it is, a smell of damp and decay pervades the interior. On my last visit a pigeon – Venice's most harmful enemy if we discount the pollution from Mestre and the teenagers – was flying from one end to the other while its mates were complacently cooing from the cornices. And no wonder. I soon discovered how they got in. In speculating why I was chilled to the marrow by an icy blast and why the tattered blind of a clerestory window was waving horizontally from the north transept, I noticed a thick crack, through which daylight was perceptible, running from one of the great single-handled stucco urns above the cornice down to the ground. 'I do not think the cry of seagulls on a gloomy day is a joyous sound', W. D. Howells complained after he had visited the Gesuiti. I know how he felt having myself often been the only person in the church on a winter afternoon when gusts of wind from the Alps and a drenching drizzle are wafted across the grey lagoon.

One senses that the Gesuiti must be a burden almost too much for Venice to bear, standing as it does on a limb, little visited by tourists and little frequented today by worshippers. How can the Church and the Belle Arti afford to maintain it? The very weight of the ubiquitous marble must be too great for the foundations, judging by the undulating polychrome pavement at the north-west corner of the nave. This subsidence, which in St Mark's contributes to the medieval and Byzantine antiquity of the basilica, is a little unseemly in a classical fane.

The barrel-vaulted ceiling over the nave is magnificently decorated in gilded compartments by a stuccoist called Abbondio Stazio. It has two large painted panels, both relating to Abraham and his exploits – not, as one might expect, to St Ignatius Loyola. They are in fresco by Francesco Fontebasso. This artist, born in the first decade of the eighteenth century, came under the influence of Sebastiano Ricci and in the 1760s was lured to St Petersburg by Catherine the Great. There is a third, circular panel over the crossing, *The Celestial Symphony*, and a fourth, also circular, *The Glory of the Name of Jesus*, in the presbytery saucer dome. Likewise in fresco they are painted by Louis Dorigny, a Frenchman who was a pupil of Charles Lebrun, the academic artist who became *premier peintre* to Louis XIV at the Gobelins factory and himself studied under Poussin.

Above the main door on the west wall is a colossal monument to three late sixteenth-century procurators of the Da Lezze family. The central portion consists of two orders supporting a sarcophagus and three busts commemorating the deceased, of which the central to Priamo Da Lezze is by Vittoria. The whole affair was designed by Sansovino and is a survival from the previous church.

On either side of the nave are three altar chapels connected by large portals with gold curtain boxes intended for real curtains which have long since perished. In the third chapel on the right Antonio Balestra's canvas (dated 1704) commemorates that very popular youth in Jesuit circles, Stanislas Kostka, whose ravishing tomb with recumbent effigy occupies a chapel dedicated to him in Sant'Andrea al Quirinale, Rome. The son of a Polish senator, he longed to become a Jesuit but his father violently opposed it. So he set off on foot through Germany to Rome where St Francis Borgia received him. He died after a nine-month novitiate in a state of phenomenal piety, beloved by all, at the age of eighteen. Here he is depicted in the clouds holding the infant Christ while the Madonna, supported by angels, stretches out her hands apprehensively, and St Francis Borgia below looks rather shocked by the liberty his young protégé is taking. The theme was a bold one for an artist to adopt even in Baroque times.

In the right transept is the splendiferous altar of St Ignatius under a pointed and curved double pediment. It is richly marbled, a work 'of cold, accurate execution' (says Lorenzetti). The saint's statue is by Pietro Baratta, a Florentine who worked for Bernini.

On each of the four piers of the crossing where nave, presbytery and transepts meet is a statue of an archangel by Torretti. These figures of Michael, Gabriel, Raphael and Sealtiel are possibly the most beautiful Rococo statues by a

Venetian sculptor and must on no account be overlooked. St Michael, in the process of spearing his victim, wears a helmet with a gallant spray of plumes as feathery as the tips of his wings. The folds of his cloak palpably vibrate with the energy of his action in ridding the earth of 'that old serpent called the Devil and Satan'. Would that he had been more successful! St Gabriel is hardly less heroic, but his attitude is more conventional than the other's. St Raphael the healer was an altogether gentler character. We see him leading by the hand the boy Tobias. St Sealtiel, with whom I must confess to being unfamiliar, is the least lively of the four figures. It is strange that the flamboyant Torretti should have been the first teacher of the cold and classical Canova.

Before you study the high altar I feel constrained to mention in passing the Baroque monument in the chapel to the right of the presbytery. It was erected by the Senate to commemorate after his death in 1675 the heroic conduct of Orazio Farnese, a Venetian captain, during the prolonged battle of the Dardanelles against the Turks.

The Manin family did the Jesuits and themselves proud with the high altar. It is a Rococo version in miniature of Bernini's famous *baldacchino* in St Peter's, Rome. A forest of twisted columns of *verde antico* supports an entablature of rippling concavities. From it rises on scrolled trusses, which form a segmental arch, a cupola, shaped like the half of an egg and perforated in a scale pattern. The cupola carries a finial. This gorgeous canopy was designed by Giuseppe Pozzo, a barefoot lay Carmelite, thought to be a brother of the famous Padre Andrea Pozzo, painter of the vast ceiling of Sant'Ignazio, Rome. One wonders how and why these brothers with their uncontrollable imaginations and love of splendour and gaiety, who one supposes would have been happier indulging in the frivolities of the carnival rather than the austerities of the cloister, ever came to enter holy orders. The canopy shelters a stupendous altarpiece by Torretto, aided by Fattoretto. It consists of a white marble globe on which God the Father and the Son, holding an immense cross, sit precariously side by side, their only visible support being the head of a *putto* under a thigh.

Two winged angels, holding hands, somehow manage with a great fluttering of wings and sprawling of naked legs to carry the weight of globe and deity. Below this group is the tabernacle proper, an architectural structure in miniature of two orders, encrusted with lapis lazuli. Two beautiful little archangels between the damask patterned columns of the apse are also sculpted by Torretto. It is interesting to venture, if nobody is about, behind the *baldacchino* to see how unfinished and sad it is at the rear. When I ventured there was a pathetic little bunch of fading carnations in a tooth tumbler beside the old cupboard in which the priest keeps the sacramental oil.

Over five steps to the altar is laid the marvellous Turkey carpet, made of marble, and creased at the corner of each step as a carpet made of real stuff would be. Needless to say, within the altar rails is the family sepulchre of the Manins. They would not be pleased by the ignoble little modern altar which has been erected over them, as though deliberately. It is a familiar case of putting down the mighty from their seats without exalting anybody of low degree.

To the left of the high altar and framing the sacristy door is a striking monument to *Doge Pasquale Cicogna* lying asleep on his elbow, a hand curved under his cheek from which flows a long beard. This pre-Baroque sculpture, the work of Gerolamo Campagna at the end of the sixteenth century, is another left-over from the previous church. It is a fine monument to a doge whom the Venetian people regarded as God-given and who was responsible for the building of the Rialto Bridge.

In the altar of the left transept hangs a large Tintoretto of *The Assumption*, originally painted for the high altar of the old church of the Crociferi. It is a youthful work and much overpainted. High above the arch leading to the three northern chapels the organ loft, its projecting balustrade of marble like that of a royal pew, balances its fellow overlooking the south transept.

Continuing anti-clockwise, as is the wont of Italian guide-book directions, you pass a conventional Mannerist-style altar enclosing a statue of the *Virgin and Child* signed by Andrea dell'Aquila da Trento who joined Vittoria's workshop in 1578.

You will do better to spend time on Titian's *Martyrdom of St Lawrence* in the chapel nearest the west entrance. It is one of Titian's great paintings although difficult to see owing to two factors. One is the dark corner in which it is situated and the other its being a chiaroscuro painting – that is to say in a low key, depicting a nocturnal scene by torchlight – incidentally the first known experiment of the sort – which has moreover suffered damage over the centuries. Titian finished it in 1558 in honour of his friend Lorenzo Massolo. It had considerable influence upon the school of Caravaggio and the Tenebrists of the seventeenth century. It is a very terrible picture, the horror of the scene made worse by the beauty of the temple architecture in the background and the classical urn in the foreground. By the light of flames from torches on poles, and a celestial ray breaking through clouds upon the principal actor in the drama, you see St Lawrence lying on a grid of red hot fuel. A man is poking him as though he were a faggot with a two-pronged fork. W. D. Howells, who saw the painting on a bitterly cold day, felt envious of the saint toasting so comfortably 'amid all that frigidity'. He pointed out that in Venice post-Renaissance churches were in winter the coldest places imaginable, colder than out of doors. Peasant women in the mid-nineteenth century took with them a *scaldino*, or pot of burning charcoal, on which to warm their chapped and chilblained fingers. The men went out of doors during the sermon to get warm.

My complete loneliness was broken by the unexpected presence of the church's old *custode* at my side. He found me admiring the confessionals which like so many in other Venetian churches are simple but handsome objects of joinery. These are presumably coeval with the building. Instead of being disdainful he was pleased. Could they be made of walnut, I asked? '*Si, si, tutti di noce*', he said. Every piece of furniture in Italy was made of walnut in the old days, he assured me. But now every walnut tree in the country had been cut down. Everything good and beautiful was, if not extinct, then in the process of being extinguished. He was a man after my own heart. He heaved a great sigh. I was amazed that an old man who sold rather indifferent picture postcards and no guide-book, should be aware of, let alone mind such things. '*Si, si,*' he repeated, '*è la rovina del mondo, del bel' mondo.*' I was so moved that I bought every postcard he had in his scruffy glass-topped box. '*Grazie, e buona sera, signore,*' he said with that proud courtesy which Italians of his generation have always shown me. '*Buona sera.*'

GLOSSARY

of Architectural Terms and Italian Words (in italics)

Aedicule – a shrine that frames with columns or pilasters a doorway or niche in a temple-like fashion.

Ambone – projecting desk from which the Epistle and Gospel were read. After the fourteenth century the pulpit took over.

Ambulatory – a corridor where one walks, sometimes open and sometimes surrounding a building.

Aquasantiere – a font.

Architrave – the lowest of the three components of an entablature (frieze and cornice being the two upper components).

Assunta – the Assumption.

Atrium – a colonnaded quadrangle before a church.

Baldacchino – a baldaquin, or large canopy, often upheld by columns, over a high altar or throne.

Bay – a compartment, measured on the exterior of buildings by the number of windows; and indoors, the divisions of a room by a column or pilaster projecting from the wall.

Camerlengo – Cardinal Chamberlain to the Pope.

Campanile – church tower, often detached. That of St Mark's is always referred to as *the* Campanile.

Campo – a small square in Venice (literally a 'field').

Cappella – a chapel.

Cassone – a chest.

Ciborium – canopy, usually over an altar; smaller than a baldaquin.

Clerestory – that part of a church, often windowed, between the arch heads of the nave and the springing of the roof.

Condottiere – leader of a band of mercenary soldiers.

Console – an ornamental bracket, which supports a cornice.

Corbel – a projection from a wall supporting a superimposed weight.

Cove – a concave curved surface between the wall and ceiling of a room.

Crocket – a decorative feature on the outline of a gable or spire.

Crossing – where the transverse arms of a church meet, usually between nave and sanctuary.

Custode – the guardian of a church.

Cusp – the projecting point of a trefoil, quatrefoil, cinquefoil, etc.

Drum – the circular base, possibly niched or windowed, on which a classical dome rests.

Entablature – the upper part of an order, consisting of architrave, frieze and cornice.

Finial – the crowning ornament of a Gothic gable or canopy, often spiked.

Garth – a central open area, or garden, surrounded by cloisters.

Giant order – columns or pilasters which enclose several storeys or window levels of a building.

Iconastasis – the screen in Byzantine churches separating sanctuary from nave, priests from congregation.

Impost – the bracket or ledge from which an arch springs.

Intarsia – marquetry, or inlaid wood.

Jamb – the upright side of a doorway or window.

Lesena – a pilaster.

Lunette – a space above a doorway or window, or a window itself shaped like a half-moon.

Madonna Orant – statue of Our Lady in prayer.

a4Martyrium – a martyr's grave or tomb.

Misericord – the bracket on an upturned seat on which a monk can perch while standing in the choir stalls.

Newel – the post which marks a break in a balustrade, or the balusters of a staircase.

Ogee (*adj.* ogival) – a double curved mould, concave above and convex below.

Orto – orchard.

Parlatorio – room in a nunnery in which talking is permitted.

Parrocchia, or *parrocchiale* – a parish church.

Palo – a stake, or post, standing in the canals in front of palaces, and in the lagoons for attaching gondolas.

Pediment – the triangular feature above a doorway or crowning the columns of a portico.

Piano nobile – the first floor of a palace housing the rooms of state.

Piazza – a square. Only the square in front of St Mark's is called the Piazza in Venice. The small squares are known as *campi*.

Piazzetta – a little square. In Venice only the little squares to the north and south of St Mark's are so called.

Plinth – a projecting base on which a column or pilaster rests.

Pluteus (Latin) – a partition or panel, usually of marble or stone.

Portego – the central room, usually from front to back of a Venetian palace.

Portico terreno – ground floor of a palace on the water level.

Predella – literally a praying stool; or reredos of a side chapel.

Presbytery – part of the church, east of the choir, where the altar stands, reserved for the presbyters.

Proto – foreman or architect who maintains a church or cathedral.

Pulvinated – applied to a mould, or frieze which is convex, or cushioned.

Putto – a cherub, or naked boy.

Quadripartite – a vault so groined as to form four partitions.

Ridotto – a gaming room.

Rio – a small canal.

Salizada – paved shopping street.

Salotto – sitting-room or small drawing-room, as opposed to *salone*, meaning the great room of a palace.

Sandalo – boat wider than a gondola.

Scalone – a staircase of a monumental kind.

Sestiere – a ward, or region of the city.

Socle – a low base supporting a statue or urn.

Soffit – ceiling, or underside of an arch.

Spandrel – the triangular space between two arches.

Squinch – a system of small concentric arches raised one above another at the angles of a square tower in order to support a circular dome.

Stilted – refers to an arch raised from the capital, or impost, before it springs.

String course – a continuous projecting band set horizontally on a façade to give emphasis or ornamentation to a plain surface.

Tessera – a little cube of mosaic.

Tester – a canopy or sounding board above a pulpit.

Traghetto – a ferry; and a ferry boat.

Transept – transverse arms of a cross-shaped church, which meet at the crossing.

Tympanum – the space between the lintel of a doorway, or window, and the arch above it.

Vaporetto – the water bus.

Verde antico – a green mottled variety of marble.

BIBLIOGRAPHY

Beckford, William. *Dreams, Waking Thoughts and Incidents*, 1783

Beerbohm, Sir Max. 'A Stranger in Venice', in *A Variety of Things*, 1906

Bradley, John Lewis (ed.). *Ruskin's Letters from Venice 1851–1852*, 1978

Bronson, Katharine de Kay. 'Browning in Venice', *Cornhill Magazine*, February 1902

Berenson, Bernard. *The Venetian Painters* (from *Italian Painters of the Renaissance*), 1894

Brosses, Charles de (Président). *Lettres sur l'Italie*, 1885

Brown, Horatio. *Life on the Lagoons*, 1884

Brown, Horatio. *Venetian Studies*, 1887

Brown, Horatio. *The Venetian Republic*, 1902

Brown, Horatio. *In and Around Venice*, 1905

Brown, Horatio. *Venice, An Historical Sketch*, 1893

Browning, Robert. 'In a Gondola'; 'A Toccata of Galuppi's'; and selected poems.

Burns, Howard. *The Genius of Venice* (Exhibition Catalogue), 1983

Byron, George Gordon, Lord. *Childe Harold's Pilgrimage*, canto 4, i-xix; 'Ode on Venice'; and selected poems

Commynes, Philippe de. *Mémoires* (trs. A. R. Scoble), 1901–4

Coryate, Thomas. *Coryate's Crudities*, 1611 (ed. M. Strachan), 1960

Demus, Otto. *The Church of San Marco in Venice*, 1960

Dickens, Charles. *An Italian Dream*, 1846

Douglas, Hugh A. *Venice on Foot*, 1925

Goethe, J. W. *Italian Journey*, 1786–8

Grundy, M. *Venice, An Anthology Guide*, 1976

Gautier, Théophile. *Italia*, 1899

Hare, J. C. Augustus. *Venice*, 1884

Haskell, Francis. *Patrons and Painters* (Part III: *Venice*), 1963

Hewison, Robert. *Ruskin and Venice*, 1978

Honour, Hugh. *The Companion Guide to Venice*, 1965

Howard, Deborah. *Iacopo Sansovino: Architecture and Patronage in Renaissance Venice*, 1975

Howells, W. D. *Venetian Life*, 1867

James, Henry. 'Venice' in *Portraits of Places*, 1882

James, Henry. *The Wings of the Dove*, 1902

James, Henry. *Italian Hours*, 1909

Lauritzen, P. L. (with A. Zielcke). *Palaces of Venice*, 1978

Lauritzen, P. L. *Venice*, 1978

Lauts, Jan. *Carpaccio*, 1962

Lieberman, Ralph. *Renaissance Architecture in Venice, 1450–1540*, 1982

Links, J. G. *Venice for Pleasure*, 1966

Lutyens, Mary (ed.). *Effie in Venice* (Letters 1845–50 and 1851–2), 1965

Lorenzetti, Giulio. *Venezia e Il Suo Estuario*, 1956

Mann, Thomas. *Death in Venice*, 1912

Marini, P. Luciano. *The Frari's Basilica*, 1982

Monckton Milnes, Richard (Lord Houghton). *Memorials of Many Scenes* (verse), 1838

Moryson, Fynes. *The Itinerary of 1594*, 1617

Morris, James. *Venice*, 1960

Musolini, Giovanni. *The Basilica of St Mark in Venice*, 1955

Musolini, Giovanni. *Torcello*, 1964

Niero, Antonio. *The Basilica of Torcello and Santa Fosca's* (undated)

Niero, Antonio. *The Basilica of S. Maria della Salute*, 1980

Norwich, John Julius. *Venice, The Greatness and the Fall*, 1981

Pope-Hennessy, Sir John. *Italian High Renaissance Sculpture*, 1963

Proust, Marcel. *Albertine Disparue*, 1925

Régnier, Henri de. *L'Altana ou La Vie Vénitienne, 1899–1924*, 1928

Rogers, Samuel. *Italy* (poem), 1823

Ruskin, John. *The Stones of Venice*, 1851–3

Ruskin, John. *St Mark's Rest*, 1877–84

Sadea/Sansoni Editori—*I Tesori: Il Settecento a Ca' Rezzonico*, 1963

Sadea/Sansoni Editori—*I Tesori: La Basilica di San Marco*, 1966

Sadea-Sansoni Editori—*La Pala d'Oro di San Marco*

Seingalt, Jacques Casanova de. *Histoire de ma Vie*, 1960

Seymour, Charles. *Sculpture in Italy, 1400–1500*, 1966

Schulz, Anne Markham. *Nicolò di Giovanni Fiorentino and Venetian Sculpture of the Early Renaissance*, 1978

Shaw-Kennedy, R. *Art and Architecture in Venice* (Venice in Peril guide), 1972

Shelley, P. B. *Julian and Maddalo*, and selected poems

173

Stendhal. 'Sur Venise' (from *Pages d'Italie*), 1818

Stokes, Adrian. *Venice*, 1944

Street, A. E. *Memoir of George Edmund Street*, 1888

Symons, A. J. A. *The Quest for Corvo*, 1934

Toesca, Pietro and Forlati, Ferdinando. *The Mosaics in the Church of St Mark in Venice*, 1958

Touring Club Italiano (TCI). *Venezia e La Sua Laguna*, 1947

Tramontin, Silvio. *La Storia dell'Isola della Salute*, 1958

Tramontin, Silvio. *La Chiesa di Santa Maria Miracoli*, 1959

Wittkower, Rudolf. *Architectural Principles in the Age of Humanism*, 1952

Wittkower, Rudolf. *Palladio and Palladianism*, 1974

Wittkower, Rudolf. *Studies in the Italian Baroque*, 1975